A SPANISH FAMILY COOKBOOK

Hippocrene is NUMBER ONE in

International Cookbooks

A SPANISH FAMILY COOKBOOK

Favorite Family Recipes

Susan Serrano
and
Juan Serrano

HIPPOCRENE BOOKS
New York

Revised Edition, 1997.
Second printing, revised edition, 2000.

For information, address:
HIPPOCRENE BOOKS, INC.
171 Madison Avenue
New York, NY 10016

Library of Congress Cataloging-in-Publication Data
Serrano, Susan.
A Spanish family cookbook: favorite family recipes / Susan Serrano and Juan Serrano
p. cm.
Includes index.
ISBN 0-7818-0546-5
1. Cookery, Spanish. I. Serrano, Juan. II. Title.
TX723.5.S7S474 1993 93-1843
641.5946—dc20 CIP

Printed in the United States of America.

CONTENTS

Introduction: Food for Thought	7
Useful Information	14
Tapas / Appetizers	17
Sopas Y Potajes / Soups and Stews	33
Verduras / Vegetables	63
Arroz / Rice Dishes	83
Huevos / Egg Dishes	95
Pescados y Mariscos / Fish and Shellfish	105
Carnes / Meats	153
Aves y Caza / Pourtry and Game	183
Salsas / Sauces	205
Postres y Pasteles / Desserts, Cakes and Pastries	217
Wines of Spain	237
Indexes:	
Recipes—English	245
Recipes—Spanish	251

Introduction

Food for Thought

This is a book about discovery and rediscovery—the rediscovery of many culinary delights of traditional regional cooking and the seeking-out of some of the newer additions to the Spanish family cookbook. It offers a selection of recipes which ranges from the simple, rustic fare of time-honored home cooking to the delicately flavored and highly esteemed dishes of more sophisticated Spanish cuisine.

Spain's extremely diverse history, geography and climate have all contributed to her culinary charm. *Paella*, the country's so-called national dish, would hardly be what it is without the golden-colored saffron introduced into Spain around the eleventh century BC by the Phoenicians, the oil and fruit of the olive trees planted by the Romans, and the short-grain rice and lemons brought by the Arabs. The country's sun-drenched vines, orchards and vegetable gardens, as well as its rolling plains, its coastal waters and the streams of its mountain valleys are all protagonists when it comes to writing Spain's *libro de cocina*, or cookery book.

The popular fallacy that Spanish food is hot and spicy is

just that—a fallacy. In fact, Spaniards generally shun hot, piquant dishes. In all the years we have spent living and traveling in Spain, we have never been served hot chili, for example, by either family or friends, and rarely have we seen them eating such dishes. Of course, exceptions can be found to every general rule. And in this case, one exception is a very popular appetizer dish, called *gambas al ajillo,* piquant garlic shrimps or prawns (served in many bars and restaurants throughout Spain), which does call for a small amount of dried red chili pepper, but here it is the garlic which provides the dish's main flavor. However, other dishes which take the name *al ajillo* (with garlic), such as *pollo al ajillo* (garlic chicken) or *champiñones al ajillo* (garlic mushrooms), have little or no trace of chili. And on the whole, Spaniards prefer their food lightly seasoned and spices are used judiciously.

A FAMILY AFFAIR

Preparing the material for this book has been a very enlightening and enjoyable experience. Enlightening, as it gave us an understanding of the extent to which regional identity and local pride are bound up with a people's food and manner of cooking. And enjoyable, because, among other reasons, it provided us with a wonderful topic of conversation with family and friends (usually over long meals). Older members of the family, in particular, love to recall favorite dishes from their youth and to pass on tips and recipes.

My mother-in-law, who recently died at a ripe old age, kept her own *libro de recetas,* or recipe book, written in her very idiosyncratic and almost indecipherable handwriting. It contained recipes handed to her by her mother, aunts and friends—some of which (as we found to our horror when we came to translate them) were not recipes as such, but rather outlines of recipes in which ingredients were named, but rarely in exact quantities with specific cooking times and temperatures. Instructions were cryptic to say the least, very often along the lines: take some beans, a handful of rice, three spoons (no size mentioned) of sugar, the required amount of meat, a little of this, a heap of that, a dribble of sherry, a slurp of wine, etc.

Clearly, these cooks took things like this for granted and expected all women to be well acquainted with such code-words and quantities and, for the most part, they were—having absorbed this knowledge naturally while helping their mothers in the kitchen. Very often these recipes were just different versions of familiar dishes. Besides, it seems that most Spanish cooks dislike following a recipe with too much exactitude. They generally prefer a more flexible approach which allows them to be inspired by the availability of local and seasonal produce, and to use their imagination and creative skills to produce their own version of a particular dish: extemporization in Spain is obviously not confined to the guitar.

Some of these recipe sketches have been included in the book, but with explicit instructions given. In some cases, we have had to fill-in the gaps by consulting family and friends, comparing other versions and, most gratifying of all, by experimenting ourselves to discover the relevant cooking times and ingredient quantities. Of course, not all the recipes are so vague. Many, usually the less familiar ones, were given in some detail. However, one recipe we have not included was a particularly ancient one for a rustic pork dish which began with the instruction: "You get the pig and you kill it!" This selection of recipes is not merely confined to the hearty food and robust fare associated with country life. Many of the dishes included possess a subtly distinctive flavor characteristic of sophisticated traditional cuisine.

A REGIONAL AFFAIR

Spanish cuisine is still very much a regional affair, although you will find the same staple ingredients in all Spanish kitchens: olive oil, flat-leafed parsley, garlic, onions, tomatoes, lemons and wine.

The central east region of Valencia and its southern neighbor Murcia—traditionally known as Levante—is the Land of Rice and Orange Blossom. Its landscape is dotted with *planteles*, or mud-walled rice plots, and *huertas*, the lush vegetable gardens with their ingenious irrigation systems, first established by the Moors. Food here obviously reflects these regional riches and the main meal usually contains some form of rice. Particularly good is the *arroz en caldero*, in which rice is cooked in a blended fish stock and flavored with saffron. Oranges are also a regular feature of a Levantine meal—either combined with other fruits and vegetables in salads, eaten as desserts (sometimes with whipped cream), or squeezed to make an orange sauce for both fish and meat dishes.

Andalusia, in the south, which gave us the liquid-gold sherry wines and the cold salad soup *gazpacho*, is the "frying pan" of Spain in more ways than one—summer temperatures often reach the mid-40s centigrade (around 110 F.), and its cooks down the ages have, on the whole, preferred frying to other means of cooking. A plate of mixed fried fish is a great favorite, and the Andalusians' skill with the frying pan usually results in fried foods that are wonderfully light and tasty. Nowadays, however, the increasing number of calorie-conscious men and women means that grilling has become equally popular—though grilling (*a la plancha*) in Spain tends to be done on the top of the stove so that the food is cooked from underneath rather than from the top.

Bordering on Portugal, in the west, is Extremadura. This region produces some of the country's best *embutidos* (sausages), especially the red sausage known as *chorizo*. This is also hunting territory and it has an abundance of rabbit, hare, partridge and quail, but the area's great epicurean treat—not least because of its rarity these days—is the *jabalí*, or wild boar.

The central plateau region—that arid plain known as the Land of Saints and Heroes, which encompasses Old and New Castile—is renowned for its meat dishes. Particularly famous are the baby lamb and suckling pig of Segovia and the roast and grilled veal of Avila. Bean and chick-pea stews are popular across the whole of Spain, yet each region has its own speciality or local version. An example of this is the well-known *cocido madrileño*, the hearty Madrid-style chick-pea stew—a descendant of the *olla podrida*, or rotten pot, mentioned in *Don Quijote*. But it is the damp, rugged, cider-producing region of Asturias in the north west, with its high mountains and harsh winter climate, that has bequeathed the most substantial of all the country's sturdy bean stews: the famous *fabada asturiana*.

Galicia, in the extreme north west (so extreme, in fact, that before the discovery of the New World, Galicia was known as land's end, or Finisterre), also has its own robust stew called *pote gallego*. However, Galicia's glory is to be found in its *rías*. The *rías* are a geological marvel of fjord-like inlets, whereby valleys have been hollowed out of the land and invaded by the ocean. The *rías* make Galicia a fish and seafood paradise and, quite naturally, the region prides itself on the quality of its shellfish dishes. Among the most renowned are the *nécoras*, or small orange crabs, and the *percebes*, or goose barnacles, both of which are unique to that coast.

Catalonia, in the north east, with its sea and mountains, has a profusion of produce which is combined often in the most unexpected ways. Everything is used in the Catalonian kitchen, very little is wasted. In fact, it sometimes seems as though everything that is in season, either from the sea or the land, has been combined in one dish. The result of this can be culinary creations which resemble multi-colored mosaics, as in *zarzuela de mariscos,* literally operetta of seafood, or the exuberant mixed salads topped with the garlic mayonnaise called *ali-oli.*

Traveling westwards from Catalonia we encounter Aragon, Navarre and Rioja. Nowadays, Rioja is famous the world over. Its name is synonymous with wine—the substantial, smooth, full-bodied wine we have come to expect when uncorking a bottle which bears this name. Like the Rioja region, Aragon and Navarre are also watered by the Ebro, Spain's longest river. Sauces are a notable feature of the Ebro Valley area. Aragonese *chilindrón* sauces—made with tomatoes, garlic, onions, cured ham, and sweet red peppers—are the most well-known. You will find meats such as lamb, rabbit and veal cooked in *chilindrón* sauces, but it is probably the chicken dish *pollo a la chilindrón* which is the most popular. Another feature of the sauces of Aragon and Navarre is their use of melted dark chocolate in dishes such as *pichones estofados* (braised pigeon or squab in chocolate sauce). Navarre is also a fisherman's dream. The rivers and streams of its mountain valleys are home to some of the most succulent trout found anywhere and, understandably, *truchas a la navarra* (baked trout, stuffed with *serrano* ham) is one the region's specialities.

The Basque country is famed for the excellence of its food. This northern region boasts some of the finest restaurants in Spain and gastronomic societies flourish in the area. Here food is generally uncomplicated—subtlety, texture, flavor and freshness being the most important requirements. Any dish which bears the label a *la vasca* (Basque-style) is usually well worth trying.

The waters which bathe the Spanish coasts—the Atlantic, Mediterranean and the Bay of Biscay—yield an abundance of fish, which is just as well as Spaniards are among the world's biggest fish eaters. The variety and freshness of the fish displayed on the counters in the local markets and supermarkets in the coastal areas, as well as in land-locked Madrid, are truly phenomenal. Spanish cooks are indeed fortunate to have such a vast array to choose from when it comes to planning their menus. And it is not surprising that so many Spanish dishes call for a combination of different fish.

A LATE AFFAIR

Meal times are much later in Spain than in many other parts of Europe, and they are often even later in the South of Spain than in the North. This is certainly one of the things that first strikes visitors, especially those from Nordic countries, who are used to lunching around 1 o'clock and dining at 7 o'clock in the evening.

Lunch in Spain is a very relaxed, almost ceremonial, affair. It is something to be shared with family and friends, and for most Spaniards the idea of munching a sandwich alone at your desk, or in a cafeteria while staring blankly into space, strikes them with horror. Such modern-day scourges are resisted still in Spain, where lunch is either eaten leisurely at home, shared with companions, or eaten in the familiar surroundings of a friendly restaurant. Tea-time (*merienda*) is at approximately 6:30pm and dinner, which is normally a light meal, is sometime around 10:00pm, and in the summer even later. The interval between the usually light breakfast of toast or rolls and coffee at about 7 or 8 in the morning and lunch, around 2:30-3:00pm, is some seven to eight hours. No wonder the Spanish invented *tapas*, the little dishes of appetizers or snacks which fill-in between meal times, and which are found in most bars all over Spain. But the mid-morning or early evening *tapas* serve not only as pleasant appetizers. Spaniards, as a rule, do not like to drink alcohol without eating something at the same time to line the stomach. At most social gatherings the *tapas* are as important as the drinks, if not more so.

* * *

Researching and writing this book has given us tremendous pleasure. It provided us with food for thought, as well as action, in so many unexpected ways. For instance, it kindled our enthusiasm for cultivating some of our own fruit and vegetables. At the bottom of our garden we now grow peppers, onions, garlic, tomatoes (the size of small melons), eggplants/aubergines, lettuce, asparagus, peas, strawberries, melons, lemons, medlars, etc.

It has helped us keep our sanity by providing a welcome break from an academic life in which writing books on Spanish grammar and teaching and writing courses on the Spanish language are the order of the day.

But, most of all, this book gave us an excuse to "eat our way through Spain" many times—often in the course of visiting family and friends in different regions, or driving leisurely, in the summer, from the North of Spain to our home in the South, each time by a different route—each time savoring different culinary delights both old and new.

Useful Information

The information below is given as a guide for European and other readers not familiar with the American standard cup and spoon measurements. The conversion quantities are not meant to be precise equivalents, as in most cases these do not give convenient working measurements. They are rounded figures used for ease of reference.

1 cup = 1 American half-pint measuring cup
or 8 fl oz, roughly 250 ml. Thus:
¼ cup = 60 ml = 2 fl oz
½ cup = 125 ml = 4 fl oz
¾ cup = 175 ml = 6 fl oz

1 cup = 250 ml = 8 fl oz
1 tablespoon = 15 ml
1 teaspoon = 5 ml

Solid Measurements:

1 oz = 25 g
2 oz = 50 g
4 oz = 125 g
8 oz = 250 g
1 lb = 500 g

Temperatures:

	F°	C°	Gas Mark
Very cool	225	110	½
	250	130	½
Cool	275	140	1
	300	150	2
Very moderate	325	170	3
Moderate	350	180	4
Moderately hot	375	190	5
	400	200	6
Hot	425	220	7
	450	230	8
Very hot	475	240	9

TAPAS

Appetizers or Hors d'Oeuvres

Spaniards take a great deal of pleasure in getting together, either at home or at a local café, with family, friends or colleagues and sharing a drink and a mid-morning or early-evening *tapa*. And instead of going out for a full evening meal, it is not unusual for a group of friends to enjoy a lively evening *de tapeo*—going to one or more favorite bars and choosing a variety of different dishes from the *tapas* menu.

Among the most popular cold tapas are simple things such as small squares or wedges of cold Spanish omelet, a few olives and nuts, small portions of cold meats, hams or sausages and pieces of *manchego* chesse. Russian salad (*ensaladilla rusa*), stuffed eggs or baked red pepper salad with vinaigrette are also familiar features in most bars.

But a small portion of almost any dish can constitute a *tapa*. Hot *tapas* are usually served in small earthenware dishes, and these include such favorites as *gambas al ajillo* (garlic prawns or shrimps), garlic mushrooms, mushrooms in sherry sauce. Even small portions of *paella* or *carne con patatas* (meat and potato stew) may be offered as *tapas* in some bars. In fact, you will often find that many bars with restaurants attached offer a *tapa* of any dish that happens to be on that day's menu. *Tapas* are usually eaten with a slice of crusty bread or a few *picos,* small crunchy bread sticks.

Following you will find some of the most popular *tapas* and where these are small servings of dishes mentioned in the book, the page number of the recipe will be shown in the index.

ACEITUNAS / OLIVES

Olives are an indispensable accompaniment to drinks and meals in Spain. The large, strong-flavored, unstoned olives are very popular as appetizers, as well as the smaller olives stuffed with almonds, sweet red peppers or anchovies.

We like to marinate olives for 2 days or more to give them an extra zip.

Marinade for 1 lb jar of olives:

3 cloves garlic—crushed
¼ cup olive oil
1 tablespoon white wine vinegar
generous pinch cumin
½ teaspoon oregano

Drain olives of any liquid.

Combine the ingredients for the marinade and add the olives. Mix well and put into a large jar or earthenware pot. Place in the refrigerator for at least two days and stir or shake the jar once or twice a day.

Remove from refrigerator at least two hours before serving.

Variation:

Take a jar of stuffed olives (preferably stuffed with red peppers) and drain away the brine. Mix together a pinch each of tarragon and majoram, a teaspoon of wine vinegar and two whole cloves of garlic and add this to the olives in the jar. Then top up the jar with olive oil and leave to marinate for 36 hours.

ALBONDIGAS / MEAT BALLS

Albondigas—served as a main course with rice and tomato sauce—have been a family standby in Spain for years, where they seem to be a great favorite with children.

However, *albondigas* are also very popular as a *tapa* dish and are found in bars throughout the country. They are particularly useful as they may be made in advance and reheated in the accompanying sauce before serving.

Though *albondigas* are often served with a rich tomato or onion sauce, in the recipe below they are accompanied by a light, but very tasty sherry sauce.

ALBONDIGAS IN SALSA DE JEREZ

Meat Balls in Sherry Sauce

½ lb ground beef

¼ cup (about 2 oz) chopped *chorizo*, or other garlic sausage

2 teaspoons finely chopped parsley

1 small egg—lightly beaten

1 slice bread — crusts removed

salt to taste

freshly ground black pepper

pinch nutmeg

water

flour for dredging

¼ cup oil for frying

Sherry Sauce:

4 tablespoons *fino*, dry sherry
½ cup beef stock
1 teaspoon chopped tarragon
seasoning to taste

Soak the bread in a little water for a few minutes. Then squeeze off excess water.

Put the beef and *chorizo* into a mixing bowl. Add the parsley, soaked bread, nutmeg, freshly ground black pepper and salt to taste, and mix well. Add the beaten egg and stir thoroughly.

Take spoonfuls of the meat mixture and form into small meat balls.

Dredge the meat balls with seasoned flour.

Put the oil into a shallow frying pan; heat and sauté the meat balls for a few minutes until cooked and lightly browned all over.

Combine all the ingredients for the sauce in a pan and bring to boiling point. Lower heat and add the meat balls, then simmer gently for a few minutes until heated through.

Makes about 16 meat balls.

ASADILLO

Baked Peppers and Tomatoes

Asadillo may be served as a *tapa* dish or as an accompaniment to many meat and fish dishes. It is delicious hot, but many people like to eat it cold, with a little vinaigrette sauce and pieces of *manchego* cheese, accompanied by a glass of full-bodied red wine.

2 medium red peppers
3 medium ripe tomatoes—peeled
2 cloves garlic—chopped
3 tablespoons olive oil

1 tablespoon fresh parsley or tarragon
seasoning to taste

Skin the peppers by heating under a hot grill or over a gas flame until the skin starts to blister. Then peel the peppers, deseed and cut into medium-thick strips. Cut the tomatoes into medium-thick slices.

Grease an ovenproof casserole with half the olive oil. Place the tomatoes, peppers and garlic in layers in the casserole, season to taste and pour over the remaining olive oil. Sprinkle with parsley or tarragon and place in a moderately-hot oven for about 25 minutes.

Serve hot or cold with lots of crusty French bread.

Serves 4.

BUÑUELITOS / FRITTERS

Buñuelitos are delicious appetizers. They are particularly popular with our family as a pre-lunch *tapa,* when they disappear almost as soon as they are brought to the table!

BUÑUELITOS DE CAMARONES

Small Shrimp Fritters

Camarones are very tiny shrimps which can be eaten in their entirety—there is no need to peel them. If not available, ordinary shrimps/prawns may be used. These should be peeled, cooked and cut into small pieces.

Batter:

½ cup all-purpose flour
generous pich salt
½ teaspoon baking powder
1 egg—lightly beaten
½ cup water

Filling:

½ cup (approx. 4 oz) baby shrimps/prawns
1 tablespoon finely chopped parsley
freshly ground black pepper
¾ cup olive oil for frying

Sift the flour, baking powder and salt into a mixing bowl. Stir in the lightly beaten egg, add the water and mix well. Cover and allow the batter to chill in the refrigerator for about one hour.

Then add the shrimps or shrimp pieces to the batter, together with the chopped parsley and ground pepper and mix well. Heat half the oil in a shallow frying pan and when hot add a tablespoon of the shrimp batter. Fry for a couple of minutes on each side, until the fritter is golden brown and crispy.

The fritters may be fried 3 or 4 at a time, depending on size of pan.

The oil will be absorbed during cooking, so add a little of the remaining oil to the pan from time to time.

Makes between 15 to 20 fritters.

Alternative Fillings:

Many different types of fish can be used instead of shrimps; cooked salt cod or tuna are very tasty alternatives.

Another very delicious variarion of *buñuelito* is one made with *serrano* ham and toasted chopped almonds.

The batter is as for shrimp fritters, but instead of fish, substitute ¼ cup (1 oz) of toasted chopped almonds and ¼ cup (2 oz) chopped ham (if *serrano* is not available, other cured ham may be used). Then make as for fish fritters.

ENSALADILLA DE NUECES

Walnut Salad

We were first served this refreshing and crunchy salad

many years ago by an aunt who lived in the beautiful village of Arcos—one of the white villages of the Cádiz Sierra. It was served as a mid-morning summer *tapa*, accompanied by a glass or two of chilled *amontillado*, or medium sherry. Since then it has been a great summer favorite of ours. The distinctive flavors of the apple, fennel and coriander combine to produce a very original and tempting appetizer.

8 walnuts—shelled
1 apple—peeled and cored
1 stalk each of fennel and celery—washed and trimmed
2 potatoes—cooked
1 cup mayonnaise
1 tablespoon green coriander—chopped

Dice the apple, fennel, celery and cooked potatoes. Combine these with the walnuts and the mayonnaise and mix well. Sprinkle with chopped coriander and serve.

ENSALADILLA RUSA
Russian Salad

This *tapa* dish, with a very un-Spanish name, is in fact one of the most popular appetizers in Spain and is found on the tapa counters of most bars. It is often served with a stuffed egg, or a tiny portion of roasted red peppers in vinaigrette.

½ cup mayonnaise
Cooked vegetables as follows:
2 potatoes—diced
2 carrots—diced
½ cup green beans—cut into small pieces
½ cup peas

Make the mayonnaise as indicated on p. 208 or use

prepared mayonnaise. Combine the cold diced cooked potatoes, carrots, the green beans and peas. Add the mayonnaise and mix well. Refrigerate for an hour and serve.

GAMBAS AL AJILLO

Garlic Shrimps/Prawns

Gambas al ajillo is probably the most well-known *tapa* dish, popular throughout the whole of Spain. Many restaurants also serve it as a first course. It should be served piping hot with lots of crusty bread, to mop up the *ajillo* sauce. A small portion of *zanahorias aliñadas* (carrots in vinaigrette dressing) seems to combine very well with this dish.

1 lb peeled raw shrimps/prawns (cooked shrimps may be used if raw shrimps are not available)
5 cloves garlic—chopped
1 small hot dried red chili pepper—seeded and chopped
good pinch salt
1½ teaspoons paprika
ground black pepper
6 tablespoons olive oil
1 lemon

If frozen shrimps are used, these should be defrosted and drained thoroughly.

Put the oil into a large, heavy frying pan or earthenware dish and sauté the garlic for a couple of minutes. Add the shrimps and stir well. Then add the chili, salt, pepper and paprika, stir and sauté for about 5 minutes, or until the shrimps are cooked and pink in color. (If cooked shrimps are used, sauté for about 2 minutes.) Sprinkle liberally with lemon juice, and serve piping hot in earthernware dishes, accompanied by crusty French bread.

Serves 4 as a first course or 6 as a *tapa*.

HUEVOS RELLENOS
Stuffed Eggs

Again, this is a familiar feature on the *tapa* counters of most bars. It is a very versatile *tapa* as the filling lends itself to many variations. It is delicious accompanied by a small dish of chilled peppers in sweet pickle, and a glass of *amontillado* sherry.

6 hard-boiled eggs
2 tablespoons mayonnaise, or heavy cream
seasoning to taste
1 teaspoon anchovy extract/essence
6 stuffed olives

Halve the eggs and remove the yolks. Sieve the yolks into a bowl and stir in the cream or mayonnaise, anchovy extract and seasoning. Mix to a smooth paste, then pipe the mixture back into the egg white halves (or use a small spoon to re-fill the egg whites). Cut the stuffed olives in half and decorate each egg with half an olive.

PIMIENTOS FRITOS
Fried Green Peppers

Pimientos fritos are served both as a *tapa* and as an accompaniment to many other dishes. The green peppers used for this dish are not the large, beefy peppers used in stews and casseroles, but the slender, sweeter and more finely textured, elongated variety. There is no need to peel or deseed the peppers. They are fried whole, sprinkled with salt and eaten with the fingers.

8 small, elongated, sweet green peppers
4 tablespoons olive oil
sea salt to taste

Wash and dry the peppers on a paper towel. Put the oil into a large frying pan and heat. Add the peppers and fry them gently over moderate heat, turning occasionally, until the peppers are cooked and lightly browned. Sprinkle with sea salt and serve immediately.

PINCHOS / MINI KEBABS

Pinchos (or sometimes *pinchitos* in Andalusia) are small cubes of meat, ham or fish which are marinated and served on a skewer together with pieces of onion and red or green peppers or tomatoes. Alternatively, the *pinchos* may be brushed with the marinade and barbecued.

PINCHOS DE CERDO

Mini Pork Kebabs with Peppers and Onions

½ lb pork loin—cut into small cubes
1 medium onion—cut into pieces for skewering
1 red pepper—cut into pieces for skewering

Marinade:
1 tablespoon olive oil
1 tablespoon wine vinegar
3 tablespoons water
pinch cumin
pinch powdered saffron
1 teaspoon thyme—chopped
seasoning to taste

Combine the ingredients for the marinade. Add the pieces of pork and marinate overnight.

Use small skewers and thread alternately with small

pieces of pork, onion and pepper. Continue until all the meat and vegetables have been used.

Put the *pinchos* under a hot broiler and cook until meat is golden brown, turning the skewers occasionally to ensure the meat is completely cooked.

Makes 6 to 7 kebabs.

Variation:

Use small pieces of chicken breast or lamb instead of pork.

The same marinade may also be used for fish *pinchos.* A good, firm-textured fish like swordfish, monkfish or shark should be used. Follow the instructions as for pork *pinchos.*

BOCADITOS DE QUESO

Cheese Bites

Bocaditos de queso are easy to make and are delicious when accompanied by a glass of chilled *fino,* dry sherry.

1 package cream cheese (3 oz size)
6 anchovy-stuffed olives—chopped
½ cup (2 oz) chopped mixed nuts
seasoning to taste
1 tablespoon milk

Put the cheese into a mixing bowl, add the chopped olives, seasoning to taste and mix well, adding a little milk to form a smooth but firm paste. Take a heaped teaspoon of the mixture and form into a small ball, then roll the cheese ball in the chopped nuts to coat. Continue until all the cheese mixture is used, then chill the cheese balls in the refrigerator for about 1 hour before serving.

Makes about 12 cheese balls.

SARDINAS ASADAS
Grilled Sardines

Although the usual translation of *sardinas asadas* is grilled sardines, the word *asado* or *asada* (from *asar*) usually refers to cooking done over an open fire. It is not surprising therefore that *sardinas asadas* are often cooked on the barbecue and served as a tasty appetizer at the start of a relaxing outdoor, summer lunch.

4 large (8 medium) sardines
sea salt
lemon wedges

Heat the grill. Wash and clean the sardines, then dry on a paper towel. Sprinkle the sardines generously with sea salt, place under a hot grill and cook about 3-4 minutes on each side, until the skin starts to burn and blister.

Remove the fish and serve with lemon wedges.

Delicious eaten with a serving of *asadillo* and a glass of *fino.*

Serves 4.

ZANAHORIAS ALIÑADAS
Carrots in Vinaigrette Dressing

Zanahorias aliñadas are a firm family favorite. Served chilled and topped with 3 or 4 chopped anchovy fillets or a little diced mountain ham, this makes a very tasty and refreshing *tapa*—it is especially good accompanied by a glass of sparkling wine or dry cider.

5-6 carrots
salt to taste

Vinaigrette:

½ tablespoon wine vinegar
2 tablespoons olive oil
2 cloves garlic—chopped
½ teaspoon chopped tarragon
1 teaspoon chopped fresh parsley
few drops lemon juice
seasoning to taste

Peel and cut carrots into chunky pieces. Boil in salted water for 5 minutes, then drain immediately. Rinse in cold water and drain again. Mix all the vinaigrette ingredients and stir well. Pour the vinaigrette over the carrots at least one hour before serving.

TAPAS EN ESCABECHE / PICKLE TAPAS

Although these pickle *tapas* are very popular, they are eaten in very small quantities as many Spaniards find them rather strong.

PEPINOS Y ZANAHORIAS EN ESCABECHE DULCE

Cucumber and Carrots in Sweet Pickle

This is often served as an accompaniment to cold roast pork or with cheese on a small square of bread.

1 cucumber—peeled and sliced
½ onion—sliced thinly
2 carrots—peeled and sliced
1 teaspoon salt

Pickle:

pinch mustard seed
pinch ground mace
½ teaspoon paprika

¼ teaspoon celery seed
½ cup sugar
¾ cup wine vinegar

Put the vegetables in a bowl and stir in the salt. Cover and set aside for a couple of hours. Then rinse thoroughly with cold water and drain.

Put spices, vinegar and sugar into a pan and bring to boil. Add the vegetables and boil for a couple of minutes. Allow to cool, then transfer to a bowl, cover and refrigerate for 24 hours. Just before serving add two finely chopped cloves of garlic.

(If preferred, a larger quantity may be made and stored in a screw-top jar.)

PIMIENTOS EN ESCABECHE DULCE
Peppers in Sweet Pickle

This is ideal as an accompaniment to cold ham.

3 medium onions—chopped
3 green peppers—chopped
3 sweet red peppers—chopped
3 cups white wine vinegar
1 teaspoon salt
1½ cups sugar
pinch mustard seed
¼ teaspoon ground black pepper

Douse the peppers and onions in a pan of boiling water and drain immediatley. Then put the peppers and onions in a saucepan containing cold water and bring to a boil. When boiling point is reached, remove the pan from heat and drain at once.

Put the sugar, salt, vinegar, black pepper and mustard

seed in a saucepan and bring to the boil. Stir in the peppers and onions and boil for two minutes. Then remove from heat, allow to cool and chill overnight.

(As in the previous recipe, if these are not eaten immediately, they may be stored in a tightly closed jar.)

OTHER POPULAR *TAPAS*

As mentioned earlier, a small portion of almost any dish can constitute a *tapa* in Spain, particularly in Andalusia. The *tapas* listed below are among the most popular and you will find the recipes for these, along with many other well-known dishes, in the relevant section of the book.

Calamares en su tinta / Squid in Its Own Ink Sauce
Callos / Stewed Tripe
Carne con patatas / Meat and Potato Stew
Champiñones al jerez / Mushrooms in Sherry Sauce
Champiñones al ajillo / Garlic Mushrooms
Paella
Pimientos asados con vinagreta / Baked peppers with Vinaigrette
Tortilla / Spanish Omelet

SOPAS Y POTAJES

Soups and Stews

GAZPACHO

The origin of this strange word *gazpacho* is uncertain. It probably derives from the pre-Roman and old Spanish word *caspa*, meaning small pieces, fragments or left-overs. The word *caspa* is thought to have been modified to *gazpa* by the Mozarabs (the Christians who lived in Arab communities in medieval Spain) in Andalusia. This explanation would fit in with what is immediately recognizable as being a major feature of *gazpacho*—the accompanying dishes of small pieces of crispy fried bread and diced vegetables, which are sprinkled on top of the soup.

In Andalusia during the summer months a large bowl of *gazpacho*, or cold salad soup, is almost a permanent feature on the table at lunch time. It is served in a cup, a glass or a bowl—usually as a starter, but it is often consumed throughout the meal as a refreshing drink instead of, or as well as, water and wine.

As with *paella*, there are innumerable recipes for *gazpacho*. Every household has its own particular favorite: some like to use wine vinegar, others prefer a combination of vinegar and lemon juice; some like a thick, strong version, others prefer to add more water in order to give a thinner, weaker consistency. Again, although the basic ingredients are tomatoes, onions, garlic, bread, oil, etc., the quantities used vary according to individual taste.

GAZPACHO ANDALUZ
Andalusian Cold Salad Soup

This is our favorite version of *gazpacho* which in the hot summer months appears on the table daily.

1 small onion
1 cucumber
1 green pepper
6 medium-large, ripe tomatoes—peeled and seeded
1 clove garlic
2 cups coarse breadcrumbs
¼ cup olive oil
3 tablespoons white wine vinegar
4 cups cold water
salt to taste
ice cubes

Garnish:

Finely chopped onion, peppers, cucumber, cured ham, fried bread cubes, etc., served in separate dishes.

To make the soup:

Chop the onion, cucumber, pepper, tomatoes and garlic, then mix together with the breadcrumbs, salt, vinegar, oil and water. Put the ingredients into a blender or processor and blend to a smooth purée. Transfer to serving bowl and place in refrigerator for about 2 hours. Just before serving, add a few ice cubes (and a little more water if desired) and stir well.

The garnishes, consisting of bowls of chopped peppers, tomatoes, cured ham, cucumber, fried bread cubes, etc., are passed around and added to the *gazpacho* according to individual preference.

Serves 6 to 8.

GAZPACHUELO CALIENTE DE PESCADO
Hot Fish Gazpacho

Normally, the word *gazpachuelo* refers to a hot soup containing beaten egg yolks, to which the egg whites are added separately and cooked until just set. However, in this Andalusian version of an ingenious and unusual fish soup, the eggs are incorporated via the mayonnaise which is added towards the end of the cooking process. The soup is then served piping hot with added *migas*, or croutons.

1 lb white fish (e.g., cod, hake, monkfish)
3 medium potatoes—peeled and cut into medium slices
2 tablespoons white wine
1 small onion
6 cups water
seasoning to taste
1 bay leaf
1 cup of mayonnaise (see p. 208)
migas or croutons (see p. 50)
1 cup clams—well scrubbed (optional)
1 tablespoon chopped parsley

Put the water, seasoning, onion (cut into quarters), bay leaf, white wine and cleaned fish into a saucepan and bring to boil. Cover and simmer for 10 minutes, then remove from heat, and set aside. (If clams are used, they should be cooked separately—following the instruction on p. 127—and the cooking liquid passed through a fine sieve or muslin to remove any sand. The strained clam liquid should then be added to the fish in the saucepan.)

Strain most of the cooking broth from the fish into another saucepan, reserving just a little to prevent the fish from becoming dry. Add the peeled, sliced potatoes to the broth, cover and allow to cook gently for 20-30 minutes. Add a little more water if necessary. When cooked, remove the potatoes and keep hot.

Cut the fish into small pieces (having removed any skin or bones), and set aside.

In a large soup tureen first put the mayonnaise and, little by little, pour in the hot fish broth, stirring constantly. Then add the fish, potatoes, parsley and clams (if used).

Serve and add the *migas* or croutons to the individual soup bowls.

Serves 6.

GAZPACHO CALIENTE GADITANO

Hot Gazpacho, Cadiz-style

Cádiz is the oldest inhabited city in the Western world. Its original name was Gadír, meaning walled enclosure. The maritime tradition of this city dates back to its original founders, the Phoenicians—a seafaring people who founded Gadír as a trading post in 1100 BC. The city's original name is still encountered in modern-day Spanish in the word *gaditano* which refers to a person or thing that comes from Cádiz.

This hot vegetable soup from Cádiz could not be simpler to make. It is nourishing and filling, and is ideal as a first course of an informal winter lunch.

4 medium-large, ripe, tomatoes—peeled and chopped

4 cloves garlic—skinned and crushed
1 large sweet red pepper—seeded and chopped
1 green pepper—seeded and chopped
1 teaspoon paprika
3 tablespoons olive oil
1 cup coarse breadcrumbs
4 cups vegetable stock
seasoning to taste
1 tablespoon chopped parsley
freshly ground black pepper

Combine the tomatoes, garlic, peppers, paprika and oil in a food processor and blend until smooth. Add this to the vegetable stock and the breadcrumbs, check for seasoning, then heat in a saucepan. Serve immediately in individual bowls, and sprinkle with parsley and freshly ground black pepper.

Serves 4 to 6.

SOPA DE AJO BLANCO CON UVAS

Cold Almond, Garlic and Grape Soup (Also called White Gazpacho)

Although this delicately flavored cold soup has been served in Andalusia for years, it seems to be experiencing something of a revival at the moment, being particularly popular for summer lunch parties.

1 cup (4 oz) chopped, blanched almonds
2 cloves of garlic—chopped
3 tablespoons sunflower oil
2 tablespoons wine vinegar
4 slices of bread, crusts removed (about 4 oz)
1 generous cup sweet grapes—peeled, destoned and halved
1 cup water—to soak bread

5 cups iced water
seasoning to taste

Put the bread into a bowl, pour over one cup of water and leave to soak for about 20 minutes, then drain and squeeze out excess water. Mix together the bread, chopped garlic, salt and almonds. Then, slowly incorporate the oil, stirring continuously and, finally, stir in the vinegar.

Put the mixture (in batches if necessary) into an electric food processor or blender and process into a smooth, light paste. When blended, gently stir in the iced water (according to consistency desired) and mix well. Strain the cold soup through a wire sieve into a large serving bowl and place in the refrigerator for an hour or so.

Before serving, mix well, add a little more iced water if necessary and add the grapes.

Serves 6.

SOPA DE AJO SENCILLA

Simple Garlic Soup

There are several amusing colloquial expressions in Spanish which make use of the word *ajo* (garlic), all of which stress the essential role that garlic plays as a staple ingredient in Spanish cooking, and therefore in Spanish life. Among the most familiar sayings are: *revolver el ajo,* which literally translates as "to stir the garlic," but figuratively it means "to stir up trouble"; *soltar ajos y cebollas* (literally "to release garlic and onions") means "to swear" or "to curse"; but perhaps the most common expression using *ajo* is the delightful *estar en el ajo,* which literally means "to be in the garlic," but which actually means "to be in the know." One can imagine this colorful phrase deriving from the fact that garlic is used to flavor so many dishes in Spanish cuisine that it has "inside information" on everything that is going on.

This *sopa de ajo sencilla* from New Castile is one version of numerous regional recipes for a rustic garlic soup—a common feature on so many Spanish tables.

4 slices day-old crusty white bread, coarsely crumbled (about 2 cups)
4 cloves garlic
¼ cup olive oil
1 tablespoon chopped parsley
6 cups water
2 vegetable stock cubes
good pinch cumin
1 teaspoon paprika
salt to taste

Heat the oil in a large pan, add the peeled garlic cloves and cook for a couple of minutes until soft, then crush the garlic with a fork or wooden spoon. Coarsely crumble the bread, stir in and cook until golden brown. Lower the heat and add the paprika, cumin, stock cubes, water and salt to taste. Cover and allow to simmer for 15 minutes.

Garnish with freshly chopped parsley.

Serves 6.

SOPA DE AJO CON HUEVOS (1)

Garlic Soup with Eggs (1)

This is a traditional, rustic soup in which a raw egg is added to the hot broth and is then cooked for a couple of minutes until the yolk is just set. *Sopa de ajo con huevos,* served with lots of crusty bread, often forms part of a light, but nourishing winter supper.

4 slices day-old French-style bread, coarsely crumbled (about 2 cups)

4 cloves garlic
1 small onion—chopped
¼ cup olive oil
1 tablespoon chopped parsley
1 teaspoon paprika
good pinch cayenne pepper
6 cups water
1 chicken stock cube
6 eggs
salt to taste

Heat the oil in a large pan and the garlic cloves and the chopped onion and cook until soft, then crush the garlic cloves with a fork or wooden spoon. Stir in the coarsely crumbled bread and cook until golden brown. Lower the heat and add the paprika, cayenne pepper, stock cube, water and salt. Allow to simmer for 15 minutes.

Ladle the soup into individual earthenware dishes, break one egg into each dish, sprinkle with salt and parsley, and put into a moderate oven for about two minutes, until the eggs are just set. Serve immediately.

Serves 6.

SOPA DE AJO CON HUEVOS (2)

Garlic Soup with Eggs (2)

As Garlic Soup with Eggs (1), but use 3 well-beaten eggs instead of 6 whole eggs.

Proceed in the same way, but after the soup has simmered for 15 minutes, remove from heat and, very slowly, pour in the beaten eggs—stirring constantly. Add the parsley, return pan to very low heat for a couple of minutes, still stirring, but do not allow to boil. Serve immediately.

Serves 6.

SOPA DE ALMEJAS
Clam Broth

This is just one of the many versions of a thin and not very strong clam soup found all over Spain. Fish stock may be substituted for the vegetable stock if a fuller flavor is preferred.

2 generous cups clams—well scrubbed
5 cups vegetable stock
2 cloves garlic
1 large onion—chopped
1 tablespoon chopped parsley
2 crustless slices bread (roughly chopped)
pinch powdered saffron
pinch cayenne pepper
3 tablespoons olive oil
2 tablespoons *fino* (dry) sherry
1 clove
1 teaspoon fresh lemon juice
bay leaf
seasoning to taste

Rinse the well-scrubbed clams in several changes of cold water, making sure all the sand is removed. Drain and set aside.

In a large pan, sauté the two whole garlic cloves in the oil until soft. Then remove the garlic and set aside. Add the chopped onion, parsley and bay leaf to the oil in the pan and cook until the onion is soft. Add the water, sherry, the chopped bread and seasoning to taste, and bring to the boil.

Meanwhile, in a mortar crush the clove and the two previously cooked cloves of garlic. Add this, together with the clams, to the boiling liquid, lower the heat, cover with tight lid and allow to simmer for about 5-8 minutes until the shells have opened. Discard any dead clams that have not opened. Stir in the lemon juice and serve immediately.

Serves 4 to 6.

SOPA ANDALUZA DE CALABAZA

Andalusian Pumpkin Soup

Dar calabazas (literally "to give pumpkins") is a colorful Spanish expression which means "to fail" or "to flunk" a test. However, I am sure that anyone serving this simple but nourishing pumpkin soup would receive nothing but compliments.

During the winter months, this soup is served in many Andalusian country *ventas*, or inns, accompanied by crusty local bread.

2 lbs pumpkin—peeled and cut into chunks
2 potatoes—peeled and cut into chunks
1 large onion—chopped
4 ripe tomatoes—peeled and chopped
5 cups water
seasoning to taste
bay leaf
3 tablespoons olive oil
1 cup boiled rice
ground black pepper

Sauté the onion in the oil until soft. Put the pumpkin and potato pieces, the sautéd onions, the tomatoes, bay leaf, seasoning and water into a large saucepan and bring to boil. Then reduce heat, cover and simmer for 25 minutes.

When cooked, allow to cool and then liquify the vegetables and water in an electric blender. Put the smooth vegetable purée back into the pan and reheat. Add the rice, freshly ground black pepper and serve immediately.

Serves 6.

SOPA DE BERROS, LECHUGA Y PEREJIL

Watercress, Lettuce and Parsley Soup

This is a nourishing and versatile soup. The herbs and green vegetables used can be varied according to taste and availability, and the soup can be served hot in the winter or cold (with added ice cubes) in the summer. It can also be made in advance and reheated before serving.

2 tablespoons butter
1 large onion—peeled and chopped
2 cloves garlic—chopped
1 large head lettuce—cut into pieces
1 stalk celery—chopped
1 cup breadcrumbs (made with 2 slices bread, crusts removed)
6 cups water
1 tablespoon chopped fresh parsley
1 small bunch chopped fresh watercress (about 1 oz)
3 tablespoons light cream
seasoning to taste

Wash the lettuce and watercress and set aside. In large saucepan, melt the butter and sauté the onions and garlic for 2-3 minutes. Then add the lettuce leaves, watercress and celery little by little and mix with the onions. Pour in the water, add the seasoning to taste and bring to the boil. Reduce heat immediately, cover and simmer for about 15 minutes. Remove from heat and stir in the breadcrumbs. Allow the soup to cool, then process until smooth.

Five minutes before serving, reheat the soup. Add the chopped parsley and stir in the cream.

Serves 6-8.

Variation:

In hot weather, the soup may be served cold. In this case there is no need to reheat the soup after processing, simply place in the refrigerator for two hours to chill, then before serving add the parsley, allow to stand for 10 minutes, stir in the cream and, just before serving, add a few ice cubes.

1 teaspoon of fresh mint or basil may also be added at the same time as the parsley.

SOPA DE CANGREJO

Crab Soup

This soup from Asturias in the north of Spain is delicious hot or cold. It is simple to make and can be prepared in advance, refrigerated after the liquidizing stage and then reheated before serving, adding the crab, prawns and cream as indicated. It is especially good served with a glass of strong, sparkling Asturian cider.

1 small onion—chopped
2 tablespoons (about 1 oz) chopped *serrano* ham, or other cured ham
3 cups fish stock
2 tablespoons sunflower oil
4 ripe tomatoes—skinned and chopped
½ cup (4 oz) crabmeat
½ cup (4 oz) peeled shrimps/prawns
seasoning to taste
3 tablespoons light cream

Put the oil into a large, heavy frying pan and sauté the onion until soft. Add the chopped ham and continue cooking for another 2-3 minutes. Stir in the chopped tomatoes and fish stock. Check for seasoning, cover and simmer for about 10 minutes. Allow to cool, then process in an electric blender, or gently press through a wire sieve with a wooden spoon.

Return the broth to the pan, add the crabmeat and

shrimps and heat through, but do not boil. Stir in the cream and, if eating hot, serve immediately.

(If serving cold, allow to cool and refrigerate for at least one hour.)

Serves 4.

SOPA AL CUARTO DE HORA
"Quarter of an Hour" Soup

As the name suggests, this is so called because it takes just about 15 minutes to make what is a simple, but very tasty, rustic soup.

1 small onion—chopped
2 cloves garlic—chopped
2 tablespoons olive oil
2 ripe tomatoes—peeled and chopped
6 cups water
1 fish stock cube
2 cups mussels (or 1 large cup clams)—well scrubbed and rinsed in several waters
2 tablespoons (about 1 oz) chopped *serrano* or other cured ham
pinch ground saffron
1 cup cooked boiled rice
1 tablespoon chopped parsley
2 tablespoons *fino* (dry) sherry
1 hard-boiled egg—chopped
bay leaf
seasoning to taste

Sauté the onion and garlic in the oil until soft. Stir in the tomatoes, ham, bay leaf, parsley and cook for additional five minutes or so. Add the water, stock cube, sherry, saffron and seasoning and bring to the boil; then add the well-scrubbed mussels or clams. Cover and cook until the shells have opened (about 5 minutes).

Finally, add the cooked rice and chopped hard-boiled egg and stir well. Serve immediately.

Serves 4 to 6.

SOPA DE FIDEOS AL MINUTO

Noodle Soup "in an Instant"

This soup is a traditional stand-by used by families all over Spain, especially as a first course of a late supper.

1 onion—chopped
4 cups water
1 beef stock cube
3 tablespoons olive oil
2 tablespoons very fine noodles (vermicelli)
grated *manchego* cheese (or any other hard, strong-flavored cheese)
seasoning to taste

In a large pan, sauté the onion in the oil until soft. Add the water, stock cube and seasoning and bring to boil. Stir in the noodles and simmer until just soft (about five minutes), taking care not to overcook the noodles.

Serve in individual soup dishes and sprinkle with a little grated cheese.

Serves 4.

SOPA DE LENTEJAS A LA MADRILEÑA

Lentil Soup, Madrid-Style

Friday, traditionally a day of abstinence when meat was prohibited, used to be lentil soup day in Spain, and many Spaniards still remember (indeed, many still enjoy) the weekly *plato de lentejas,* or dish of thick lentil soup—full of vitamins and iron.

This is a substantial soup which is simple to make, and the lentils do not have to be soaked beforehand.

1 green pepper—chopped
1 large onion—chopped
1 canned sweet red pepper—chopped
1 clove garlic—chopped (optional)
½ cup chopped canned tomatoes
1 cup lentils
8 cups water
3 carrots—scraped and chopped
¼ cup olive oil
1 tablespoon all-purpose flour
seasoning to taste
bay leaf

In a large saucepan, sauté the chopped onions and peppers (and garlic, if used) until soft. Add the flour and mix well. Stir in the tomatoes, sweet red peppers, carrots, lentils, bay leaf and salt and add the water. Bring to boil, then reduce heat, cover and cook slowly over low heat for about two hours, stirring occasionally.

Serves 6-8.

Variations:

Chopped cured ham or bacon may be added at the same time as the lentils.

The soup may be served as a thick, smooth purée, in which case, at the end of the cooking time, it should be allowed to cool, then liquified and reheated before serving.

CREMA DE MELÓN

Chilled Cream of Melon Soup

This is a relatively recent addition to Spanish cuisine.

As you might imagine, the use of melon in *crema de melón* produces a distinctive, sweet-tasting soup, though the sweetness is offset slightly by the saltiness of the ham and the dryness of the *fino* sherry.

1 large (2 small) ripe melon(s)
1 pint veal stock
2 tablespoons butter
2 egg yolks
2 tablespoons light cream
seasoning to taste
¼ cup (about 2 oz) chopped *serrano*, or other cured ham
2 teaspoons chopped chervil (or parsley)
2 tablespoons *fino* (dry) sherry

Cut melon(s) in half, remove seeds and scoop out about 16 small melon balls and set aside.

Remove the remainder of the melon flesh and cut into pieces. Heat the butter in a pan and sauté the melon pieces for around 4-5 minutes. Add the veal stock and seasoning to taste, cover and allow to simmer for 15 minutes. Then remove from heat, and pass through a fine sieve or process until smooth.

Pour the melon soup back into the saucepan and, over a moderate heat, stir in the cream (do not allow to boil), and the well-beaten egg yolks, stirring constantly. Remove from heat and allow to cool. Chill for a couple of hours. Stir in the sherry just before serving.

When served, add about 4 melon balls to each individual soup dish and garnish with the chopped chervil and cured ham.

Serves 4.

SOPA DE MENESTRA CON MIGAS Y YERBABUENA

Vegetable Soup with Croutons and Mint

The word *migas* is usually translated as croutons since there is no other near equivalent for this Spanish word. However, many people believe that this translation does not do justice to real Spanish *migas*—cubes of bread which are moistened and seasoned and then fried in hot olive oil, together with a little diced cured mountain ham. *Migas* have been an essential part of Spanish cuisine since time immemorial.

The use of mint in this soup highlights the Moorish influence on Spanish cuisine, and indeed mint is used in many soup and meat dishes in Spain.

Sopa de menestra con migas y yerbabuena is one of our favorite first courses, and it also makes a delicious late-night snack.

For the Soup:

4 cups water
2 onions
4 tomatoes—peeled and chopped
2 potatoes
1 leek
3 stalks celery
1 turnip
1 parsnip
2 carrots
2 tablespoons olive oil
bay leaf
1 level teaspoon paprika
seasoning to taste
mint

Migas **(Fried Bread/Croutons):**

4 thick slices day-old country bread (*pan de pueblo*)—crusts removed
2 cloves garlic
1 tablespoon diced *serrano*, or other cured ham
1 level teaspoon paprika
seasoning to taste
pinch cumin
¼ cup olive oil
water

First prepare the *migas*, or fried bread, by cutting the bread into small chunks, then sprinkle with 1 tablespoon of water and a good pinch of salt, wrap in a damp cloth and leave overnight. (If time does not allow for this, simply sprinkle the bread with salt and two tablespoons of water, cover and set aside for half an hour).

Heat the oil in a pan and add the two cloves of garlic, sauté until golden brown, then remove the garlic and discard. Add the bread to the oil left in the pan, together with the paprika, cumin and seasoning, mix well and fry over a low heat until the bread is crisp (about 15 minutes). Add the diced cured ham and continue heating for a further 5 minutes or so.

Vegetable Soup:

Peel the vegetables and cut into pieces. Put the two tablespoons of oil into a large saucepan and mix in all the vegetables except the potatoes and tomatoes. Allow to cook for about five minutes. Add the water, bay leaf, seasoning and paprika and simmer for an additional 20 minutes, then add the potatoes and tomatoes and continue cooking for a further 20 minutes.

Serve in individual soup bowls and garnish with migas and one or two mint leaves.

Serves 4-6.

SOPA DE PATATAS
Potato Soup

Sopa de patatas is an uncomplicated, rustic soup enhanced by the addition of a little sherry and chopped fresh parsley and chervil.

1 large onion—finely chopped
6 cups chicken stock
3 tablespoons olive oil
2 tablespoons *fino* (dry) sherry
6 medium potatoes—peeled and chopped
1 tablespoon chopped fresh parsley
2 teaspoons chopped fresh chervil (optional)
seasoning to taste

In a large saucepan, sauté the finely chopped onion in the oil until soft. Add the chicken stock, potatoes and seasoning, cover with lid and bring to boil. Then reduce heat immediately and simmer gently until potatoes are cooked.

When cooked, mash the potatoes in the liquid, add the parsley and chervil and stir in the *fino* sherry. Serve immediately.

Serves 6.

SOPA DE PESCADO AL AMARILLO
Saffron Fish Soup

This is a wonderful, golden soup from Levante in the east of Spain—land of the orange blossom. The fennel, saffron, orange and fish combine beautifully to produce a delicate and original flavor.

2 large onions—chopped
1 head fennel—cleaned, trimmed and chopped
2 cloves garlic—chopped

1 lb hake (or cod, or haddock) fillet—skinned
¼ cup olive oil
1 bay leaf
½ cup dry white wine
3 cups water
grated rind of half orange
pinch ground saffron (or yellow coloring)
generous pinch dried thyme
2 tablespoons vermicelli noodles
seasoning to taste

In a large saucepan, sauté the onions, fennel and garlic in the oil until soft. Cut the fish into medium-sized pieces, and add to the onions and fennel, together with the thyme, seasoning, wine, water, saffron, orange rind and bay leaf. Cover and bring to boil, then reduce heat and cook gently for about 15 minutes.

Stir in the noodles and continue cooking for a further 10-15 minutes. Serve immediately.

Serves 4-6.

SOPA DE PICADILLO

Chicken Broth with Tidbits

The word *picadillo* refers to small pieces of anything edible. And there is a poignant Spanish expression which makes good use of the word: *hacer picadillo a alguien,* meaning "to make mincemeat of someone."

However, there is no mincemeat in this *sopa de picadillo,* which can be found on almost every restaurant menu in Spain. There are many versions of this well-loved soup. The version given here is one of the easiest and quickest to make.

5 cups chicken stock
3 small hard-boiled eggs—chopped

¼ cup (about 2 oz) diced *serrano* or other cured ham
1 cup boiled rice
1 tablespoon chopped parsley
mint leaves
seasoning to taste

Put the stock into a saucepan and bring to boil. Add the chopped eggs, ham, rice, parsley and seasoning to taste. Allow to simmer for 2-3 minutes. The soup is now ready to serve.

When serving, add one or two mint leaves to each individual soup dish.

Serves 4 to 6.

CREMA DE ZANAHORIAS
Cream of Carrot Soup

Crema de zanahorias is another winter favorite in Spain. There are numerous versions of this soup but this one, incorporating plain yogurt and lemon rind, is the one we prefer.

6 cups water
2 potatoes—peeled
1 onion—chopped
1¼ lb (about 5-6) carrots—scraped and chopped
2 ripe tomatoes—peeled and chopped
1 heaped teaspoon cornstarch/corn flour
½ cup natural yogurt
3 tablespoons olive oil
grated rind of 1 lemon
1 chicken stock cube
seasoning to taste
1 tablespoon chopped parsley

Heat the oil in a large saucepan and fry the onion until soft. Add the chopped carrots, potatoes, tomatoes, water, stock cube and seasoning. Bring to the boil and allow to simmer until the vegetables are cooked—about 25 minutes.

Meanwhile, mix the cornstarch with a little water to make a smooth liquid paste. Put the yogurt into a small pan and mix in the cornstarch. Bring to boil, stirring constantly, then allow to cook over low heat for 2-3 minutes.

Add the yogurt to the vegetables and mix well. Process in batches and then reheat just before serving. Garnish with chopped parsley and lemon rind.

Serves 6.

COCIDO

Cocido is a famous and traditional stew from the New Castile area of central Spain. It has its roots in the *olla podrida* or rotten pot mentioned in Cervantes' novel *Don Quijote.* The *olla podrida* was itself a "Christian" adaptation of the ancient Jewish dish *adafina,* a pot of stew which, on Friday night, would be left to cook very slowly over the embers to be ready for eating on Saturday. In its Christian version, pork was substituted for the hard-boiled eggs of the Jewish dish. In this way, at the time of the Inquisition, the eating of *cocido* containing pork was taken as a sign that a person was a true Christian.

The meat, vegetables and broth of the *cocido*—all cooked in one big pan—provide a nourishing and substantial meal, the eating of which can be something of a ceremony, as it is usually served in three separate courses. The first course is the soup, made from the strained broth, usually served with fine noodles. The second course consists of the chick-peas and vegetables: cabbage, potatoes, carrots, etc. This is followed by the meats: chicken, pork, sausages, beef, etc., depending on the ingredients preferred.

Nowadays, *cocido* can be as elaborate or simple as personal taste, regional produce or one's purse dictates. Not surprisingly, there are many different variations of *cocido* and every region—indeed every household—adds something of its own to produce a local or personal version of this famous *puchero* or stew.

As a general rule, the Andalusian version often contains more vegetables: celery, French beans and even rice are added, and the pork omited. The Galician *cocido* or *pote gallego,* on the other hand, invariably contains pork and usually incorporates turnips.

Nevertheless, it is the *cocido* from the Madrid area which is the best known and most representative of all, as it brings together some of the most basic ingredients from all the other regional *cocidos.*

COCIDO MADRILEÑO

(Boiled Chicken, Meat and Vegetables)

½ lb dried chick-peas
1 medium white cabbage—cut into wedges
1 small onion—peeled
4 medium carrots—scraped and halved
6 medium potatoes—peeled
2 medium leeks—trimmed, washed and halved
1 *morcilla,* or other blood sausage (about 4 oz)
4 small *chorizos,* or other garlic sausage (about ½ lb)
1 ham bone (optional)
2-3 tablespoons noodles (*vermicelli*)—cooked
2 cloves garlic—chopped
small piece bacon (about 4 oz) or *serrano* ham
1 medium chicken
1 lb beef (brisket or chuck)
14 cups water
seasoning to taste

1 bay leaf
1 tablespoon chopped parsley

Wash the chick-peas thoroughly, then put them in a large saucepan and soak overnight in well-salted water—the water should cover the peas.

The next day, drain the peas, return them to the saucepan and pour in 14 cups of fresh water. Add the chicken, brisket, ham bone, onion and salt to taste. Bring to boil, removing any scum that may form on the surface of the water. Turn the heat to low, cover and simmer gently for around 2 hours. At the end of this time, remove and discard the onion and ham bone (if used). Then add the carrots, leeks, ham, garlic, bay leaf, parsley and seasoning, and simmer for 30 minutes more.

In the meantime, prick the small *chorizos* and the *morcilla* with a fork and put them into a pan. Cover with water, bring to the boil and simmer for around 5 minutes. Then drain off the water and add the sausages to the casserole, together with the whole potatoes, cabbage and black pepper. Simmer until the chick-peas and vegetables are tender—about 30 minutes.

When cooked, remove the meat, fowl and sausage. Drain and carve into serving portions, then arrange these on a large, heated serving dish and keep hot.

Strain the liquid from the vegetables and chick-peas, or remove them with a perforated spoon. Place the chick-peas in the middle of a heated serving dish and arrange the vegetables around them. Keep the meat, chick-peas and vegetables hot while preparing and serving the broth for the first course. But do not allow the meat and vegetables to become dry—if necessary moisten them with a little of the broth.

To prepare the soup, simply reheat the liquid in the pan, add the previously-cooked noodles and seasoning to taste. Serve immediately.

Serves 6.

BERZA

Berza is one of the Spanish words for cabbage. However, in Andalusia it is also the name given to a bean and cabbage stew which is a not too distant relative of *olla podrida* or rotten pot. It used to be a regular winter favorite throughout southern Spain, but nowadays it is not so easily found, except in some family-run, country *ventas* (rustic inns) or, of course, within the local family environment.

The following recipe was handed to us many years ago by María Luisa (hence the name), an elderly cook who worked for a wealthy landowner on a large *cortijo*, or ranch, in Algeciras, southern Spain. Apparently, it was the *señor*'s favorite dish, and he would ask for it even on hot summer days. Not surprisingly, he would then need an extended *siesta*!

BERZA MARIA LUISA

Maria Luisa's Bean and Cabbage Stew with Tripe

½ lb white navy/haricot beans
½ lb red kidney beans
2 medium potatoes
4 stalks celery
1 small cabbage—cut into shreds
1 green pepper—chopped
1 large onion—chopped
1 clove of garlic—chopped
½ lb salt pork
1 lb prepared tripe
3 small *chorizos*, or other garlic sausage (about 6 oz)
½ teaspoon majoram
pinch of nutmeg
3 tablespoons olive oil

seasoning to taste
water

Soak the navy/haricot and red beans in water overnight, then drain.

Wash and trim the celery and cut the stalks into medium-sized pieces. Peel the potatoes and cut into pieces. Cut the tripe and salt pork into strips.

Put the oil in a large, heavy pot and sauté the onions, garlic and green peppers until soft. Then add the beans, tripe, salt pork, celery, shredded cabbage, herbs and seasonings. Cover with water and bring to boil. Lower heat, cover with lid and simmer for about 1½ hours, (add a little more water if necessary during cooking). Prick the *chorizos*, or substitute, and add to the casserole, together with the potato pieces and continue cooking for a further 30 minutes.

Before serving, cut the *chorizos* into small pieces and return these to the casserole.

Serves 6 to 8.

CALDO GALLEGO

Galician Bean and Turnip Soup

Another relative of *cocido*, this one is from the northwest of Spain.

½ lb white navy/haricot beans
10 cups water
½ cup (about 4 oz)) diced *serrano* ham or other cured ham
¼ lb piece of salt pork or bacon
1 onion—chopped
2 small *chorizos*, or other garlic sausages (about 4 oz)
4 turnips—peeled and diced
4 potatoes—peeled and diced
seasoning to taste

Put the beans, ham, pork, onions and salt to taste into a large saucepan and cover with water. Bring to the boil, skimming off any scum that may form. Cover and simmer for about 1½ hours. Then add the sausage, potatoes and turnips and cook for an additional 30 minutes, until beans are tender. (Add more seasoning if required.)

Remove the pork and sausages and slice. Then return these to the saucepan and stir well. Serve the soup immediately.

Serves 6.

For *pote gallego* add ½ lb of stewing veal or chicken at the same time as the beans, ham, pork and onion, and continue as above.

FABADA

Fabada is a thick, nourishing bean soup or stew from Asturias, a mountainous region of northern Spain. *Fabada* is generally thought to be *un plato fuerte*, a heavy dish, perhaps the heaviest of all Spanish dishes. This is understandable given the harsh life once endured by people living in the high mountains, in the mining valleys, and the chilly, damp fishing villages of the rugged Cantabrian coast.

As with other such dishes, many locals believe that it is much better to make the stew the day before it is to be eaten and then reheat before serving. Corn bread and sparkling dry cider (the national drink of Asturias) are the usual accompaniments of *fabada*.

FABADA ASTURIANA

Asturian Bean and Sausage Soup

This recipe calls for 1 lb of dried beans, which may be all of the same type or (as we prefer) half quantities each of broad and white kidney beans.

½ lb white kidney beans
½ lb dried broad beans
2 onions—chopped
2 cloves garlic—chopped
¼ lb piece *serrano*, or other cured ham
¼ lb piece of salt pork
1 pig's trotter
2 small *chorizos*, or other garlic sausage (about 4 oz)
1 *morcilla*, or other blood sausage (about 4 oz)
pinch ground saffron
1 teaspoon paprika
seasoning to taste
bay leaf
water

Soak the dried beans in water for at least 3 hours, or overnight.

Then drain beans and put them into a large pan and cover with water. Bring to boil and simmer for 2-3 minutes. Drain beans of all the water and return them to the pan.

Add onions, garlic, bay leaf, seasoning, paprika, salt pork and the trotter to the beans in the pan and cover with water. Bring to the boil, then reduce heat, cover, and simmer gently for around 1 hour.

Now prick the *chorizos* (or substitute red sausage) with a fork and add them, together with the ham, to the pot, and continue cooking for another hour.

Prick the *morcilla* (or substitute blood sausage) with a fork and add to the stew, together with the saffron, and continue cooking for about 30 minutes, until beans are tender.

When the soup is cooked, transfer the sausages, pork and ham onto a plate and cut into chunky pieces, then return to the soup and heat through.

Serves 6.

GUISO RAPIDO DE GARBANZOS
Rapid Chick-pea Stew

A modern, convenience version of an old Spanish *cocido*, this dish makes a substantial stew which is very appetizing on cold winter evenings. It is particularly useful when time is short, as it only takes about half an hour to prepare.

1 medium can chopped tomatoes (16 oz size)
1 can chick-peas (16 oz size approx.)
½ lb frozen green beans
1 large onion—chopped
2 cloves of garlic—chopped
1 tablespoon chopped parsley
¼ lb chopped smoked ham or bacon
2 oz *chorizo*, or other garlic sausage—diced
2 oz *morcilla*, or other blood saugage—diced
3 tablespoons oil
2 cups water
1 chicken stock cube
freshly ground black pepper
salt to taste

Dissolve the stock cube in one cup of hot water and set aside.

Open can of chick-peas, drain of liquid and set aside.

Put the oil in a large shallow pan and sauté the onion and garlic until soft. Add the green beans, chopped tomatoes, parsley, ham and diced *chorizo*. Pour in the chicken stock and the remaining cup of water and mix well. Cover and simmer for 10 minutes. Then add the chick-peas, diced *morcilla* and freshly gound black pepper and stir well. (Check whether salt is desired, as this dish usually requires little or no salt at all.) Cover and simmer for an additional 10-15 minutes, or until the beans are tender.

Serve with crusty French bread.

Serves 3-4.

VERDURAS

Vegetables

APIO EN SALSA DE TOMATE
Celery in Tomato Sauce

In Spain vegetables are rarely cooked just in boiling water and served with a main course of meat and plain vegetables. As a general rule, young seasonal vegetables are sautéed in oil until tender, or if boiled, they are then drained and lightly sautéed or baked in a little oil or butter afterwards. You will find that they are almost always combined or cooked with other ingredients and served as a separate course—often with a rich sauce.

This tasty celery dish is a typical example, and although it makes a pleasant accompaniment to meat, poultry and ham, it is usually served as a separate dish.

2 heads celery
1 medium can chopped tomatoes (16 oz size)
2 teaspoons tomato purée/paste
1 medium onion—chopped
½ cup grated cheese—*manchego*, gruyere or similar

2 tablespoons oil
2 teaspoons chopped sweet basil
seasoning to taste

Wash and trim the celery stalks and cut in half. Put the celery stalks into a pan of boiling water, cover and simmer until cooked (about 10 minutes).

Remove celery with perforated spoon and drain well. Set aside.

Sauté the chopped onion in the oil until soft, then add the tomato purée/paste, chopped tomatoes, sweet basil and seasoning, and mix well.

Place the celery in a greased, ovenproof dish and pour over the tomato and onion mixture. Sprinkle the cheese over the top, and place in a preheated, moderately hot oven for about 15 minutes, until completely heated through.

Serves 4.

BANDERA ESPAÑOLA

"The Spanish Flag"
Stuffed Red and Yellow Peppers with Tomato Sauce

This colorful dish is so named because the red and yellow (the Spanish national colors) peppers used are arranged in rows which form the same design as the Spanish flag. It can be prepared in advance and heated through in the oven before serving. It is a useful party dish, serving 8-10 people.

2½ cups cooked rice (approx. 3 tablespoons per two peppers)
8 red peppers
8 yellow peppers
4 cloves garlic—peeled and chopped
3 medium onions—skinned and chopped
3 cups mushrooms—washed and chopped
5 strips (about 6 oz) smoked bacon—chopped

½ cup canned chopped tomatoes
3 tablespoons chopped parsley
6 tablespoons olive oil
good pinch dried thyme
¾ cup vegetable stock
seasoning to taste
tomato sauce (see p. 212)

Cut off the tops of the peppers, scoop out seeds and wash peppers. Discard seeds, core and stem.

Put the peppers and the pepper tops into a large pan, cover with water containing salt to taste, bring to boil and simmer for about 15 minutes. Then remove the peppers and drain. Set aside.

Meanwhile, cut the bacon into small pieces, sauté for a few minutes and set aside.

Put the oil in a large frying pan, add the chopped garlic and onion and sauté until soft. Then add the chopped mushrooms, tomatoes, parsley and seasoning (use plenty of ground black pepper). Stir well and cook for an additional 5 minutes. Add the rice, the chopped bacon and the stock and mix well.

Grease a large rectangular ovenproof dish and arrange the peppers in the dish in rows as follows: a first row of 4 red peppers, then two rows of 4 yellow peppers and a final row of 4 red peppers, giving a total of 4 rows.

Fill the peppers with the stuffing, cover with the pepper tops and bake in a preheated, moderately hot oven for around 15 minutes, until completely heated through.

Serve with tomato sauce (see p. 212).

Serves 8 to 10.

BERENJENAS FRITAS
Fried Eggplant/Aubergine

Berenjenas fritas are often served as an accompaniment to many fish and meat dishes.

2 medium eggplants/aubergines
flour for coating
1 cup oil for frying
salt to taste

Wash eggplants/aubergines, dry on paper towel and cut off stalk.

Slice the eggplants thinly, place them on a large platter and sprinkle them with salt. Set aside for about one hour until they have given off all the water. Then dry each slice with a paper towel and dip in the flour, coating generously. Shake off any excess flour.

Heat the oil in a large frying pan and, when hot, fry the slices of floured eggplant until golden in color, turning if necessary. Keep hot. Do this in batches until all the eggplant slices are cooked.

You may want to refry rapidly the first couple of batches so that all the eggplant slices are sizzling hot. Serve immediately.

Serves 4 to 6.

BERENJENAS CON JAMON Y BECHAMEL
Eggplant/Aubergine with Ham and White Sauce

Berenjenas con jamón y bechamel may be served as a starter or part of a main course.

3 large (or 6 small) eggplants/aubergines
½ cup (about 4 oz) chopped *serrano*, or other cured ham
1 cup fresh breadcrumbs

1 medium onion—chopped
1 tablespoon chopped parsley
oil for frying
seasoning to taste

White Sauce:
1 cup hot milk
1 tablespoon all-purpose flour
1 tablespoon butter
seasoning to taste

Cut eggplants in half lengthwise, then, without cutting through the skin, make a few cuts with a knife in the eggplant flesh and sprinkle with salt. Let sit for around 30 minutes for the eggplants to give off their bitter juice.

Meanwhile, in a large shallow pan, fry the chopped onion until soft. Stir in the ham, parsley and seasoning to taste, and set aside.

To make the white sauce: Melt the butter in a saucepan over a moderate heat, mix in the flour to form a roux or paste, then gradually stir in the hot milk, add salt and pepper to taste and cook for around 5 minutes, stirring constantly, until the sauce is thick and smooth. Set aside.

When the liquid has been drawn from the eggplants, dry them with a paper towel. Heat 3-4 tablespoons of oil in a large, shallow pan and lay the eggplants (flesh-side down) in the pan. Sauté until golden brown, then turn and fry on the skin side for a few minutes. Lift eggplants out of pan and dry. Scoop out the flesh and chop. Set the skins aside.

Combine the chopped eggplant flesh with the onion and ham mixture in the large shallow pan, cover and cook for about 5 minutes. Then add the white sauce and mix well.

Put the eggplant skins on a greased, ovenproof dish and fill with the sauce mixture. Sprinkle the top with breadcrumbs and put into a preheated, moderately hot oven for around 10-15 minutes until golden brown.

Serves 6.

BERENJENAS CON SETAS Y TOMATE

Eggplant/Aubergine with Mushrooms and Tomatoes

Berenjenas con setas y tomate is a typical Mediterranean dish. In Spain, this is usually served as a first course, often with the addition of a little diced cured ham.

2 large eggplants/aubergines
2 cups (about ½ lb) mushrooms
1 medium can chopped tomatoes (16 oz size)
1 medium onion—chopped
1 clove of garlic—chopped
2 teaspoons fresh basil—chopped
3 tablespoons oil
seasoning to taste
freshly ground black pepper

Peel the eggplants and cut into good sized chunks. Put into a saucepan, cover with water, add salt to taste, and bring to the boil. Simmer gently for 15-20 minutes. Then drain.

Meanwhile, fry the chopped garlic and onion in the oil until soft. Add the mushrooms, basil and seasoning and cook for an additional 5 minutes.

Add the drained eggplant, chopped tomatoes and a little water if required. Mix well, cover and cook gently for an additional 10 minutes. Sprinkle with freshly ground black pepper and serve immediately.

Serves 4 to 6.

CALABACINES GRATINADOS

Zucchini/Courgettes Gratin

This dish, made with delicately-flavored, young zucchini/courgettes, is excellent as a first course.

6 medium-sized firm zucchini/courgettes
¾ cup grated cheese (*manchego*, gruyere, cheddar, etc.)
½ cup breadcrumbs
1½ tablespoons butter
pinch nutmeg
seasoning to taste
water

Wash the zucchini and dry with paper towel. Top and tail and cut into medium-sized pieces. Put into a saucepan. Cover with boiling water, add salt and simmer for 3-5 minutes. Then drain.

Put a layer of zucchini in a large, greased ovenproof dish, cover with half the grated cheese and sprinkle with nutmeg and seasoning. Put another layer of zucchini on top, using up all the zucchini. Cover with the remaining grated cheese, the breadcrumbs, a little more nutmeg and seasoning. Dot with butter and place in preheated, moderately hot oven for about 15 minutes until golden brown. Serve immediately.

Serves 4.

CHAMPIÑONES AL AJILLO

Mushrooms in Garlic Sauce

Like *gambas al ajillo* (garlic prawns), mushrooms in garlic sauce is a firm favorite throughout the whole of Spain as a *tapa*, or appetizer.

4 cups (about 1 lb) button mushrooms

5 cloves of garlic—chopped
1 tablespoon chopped parsley
¼ cup oil
1 teaspoon paprika
seasoning to taste

Wash the mushrooms well, or peel if preferred.

Put the oil, garlic, mushrooms, parsley, paprika and seasoning in a large, earthernware dish and mix thoroughly. Cook over medium heat for around 10 minutes. Then lower heat and cook for a further 10 minutes. Serve immediately.

Serves 4 to 6 as a *tapa* (appetizer).

CHAMPIÑONES AL JEREZ
Mushrooms in Sherry Sauce

We are fortunate enough to have access to a good quality *fino* from the family's old sherry bodega, so this is a dish which appears regularly on our table, both as a starter or a *tapa* (appetizer).

4 cups (about 1 lb) button mushrooms.
¼ cup *fino* (bone dry) sherry
1 clove garlic—chopped
1 small onion—chopped finely
pinch cumin
1 tablespoon chopped sweet basil
¼ cup oil
seasoning to taste

Wash the mushrooms well (or peel if preferred) and dry on paper towel.

Put the oil in a large frying pan and sauté the garlic and onions until soft. Add the mushrooms, basil, cumin and seasoning, stir well and cook for an additional 2-3 minutes.

Pour in the *fino* (dry sherry), cover and simmer gently for 10 minutes (add a little water if necessary). Serve immediately.
Serves 4 to 6 as a *tapa* (appetizer).

ENSALADA DE PATATAS MALLORQUINAS
Mallorca-Style Potato Salad

This delightful, rustic salad from the island of Mallorca is suitable as a first course for a summer lunch, a light evening snack or appetizer.

2 lbs potatoes
seasoning to taste
1 tablespoon white wine vinegar
1 tablespoon chopped parsley
¾ cup mayonnaise (or to taste)
3 hard-boiled eggs—sliced
1 medium can sardines in oil
4 small canned anchovy fillets—chopped
6 black olives
1 lemon

Boil the potatoes in their skins until cooked, but firm. Allow to cool.

If old potatoes are used, peel them; if using new potatoes, leave the skins on. Cut the potatoes into medium slices, put into a serving dish, add seasoning and stir in the vinegar. Add the mayonnaise and anchovies, and mix well. Then arrange the sardines, hard-boiled egg slices and olives on top. Sprinkle with parsley and garnish with lemon slices.

Serves 4 to 6.

HABAS A LA CATALANA

Broad Beans with Sausage, Catalan Style

There is a very interesting Spanish proverb which says: *En todas partes cuecen habas*, which translates literally as "beans are cooked all over [the world]," but which actually means "it's the same the whole world over." However, whether you interpret this proverb literally or metaphorically, broad beans are certainly an important feature of Spanish cusine. As in this recipe from Catalonia, they can be eaten as a hearty first course or as a main course.

1½ lb cooked broad beans
4 small *chorizos*, or other garlic sausage (about ½ lb)
½ cup (¼ lb) salt pork—diced
4 tablespoons chopped scallions/spring onions
2 cloves garlic—chopped
3 tablespoons oil
½ cup dry white wine
½ cup water
1 tablespoon chopped fresh mint
1 bay leaf
seasoning to taste
1 tablespoon chopped parsley
water for cooking *chorizo*

First cook the *chorizo* sausages: prick them with a sharp knife and put them into a pan of cold water, bring to boil and simmer for 5 minutes. Remove the sausages, drain well, and cut into medium-thick slices.

Put the oil into a large casserole and sauté the salt pork until tender. Then add the scallions and garlic and cook until soft. Stir in the wine, water, mint, seasoning and bay leaf, and add the *chorizo* sausage slices. Cover and simmer over low heat for about 15 minutes. Add the cooked broad beans and parsley and continue cooking for an additional 10 minutes. Serve immediately.

Serves 4 to 6.

JUDIAS VERDES SALTEADAS CON JAMON

Green Beans with Ham

As mentioned, green beans, broad beans, peas and artichokes, each cooked with garlic and ham, are firm favorites in Spain and are usually eaten as a starter. But they are equally good with a young chicken or an omelette as a light lunch. The ham is sometimes omitted, depending on taste and what is available.

We like to serve green beans and peas cooked in this way:

1 lb green beans—washed and trimmed
1 small onion chopped
2 cloves garlic—chopped
3 tablespoons olive oil
½ cup (about 4 oz) chopped *serrano,* or other cured ham
seasoning to taste

Put the beans in a saucepan of boiling water with salt to taste and simmer until tender, about 8 minutes. Then drain the beans and set aside.

Pour the oil into a large frying pan and sauté the onion and garlic until soft. Add the ham, beans and seasoning and stir well. Cover the pan and cook very gently for an additional 5 minutes. Serve immediately.

Serves 4 to 6.

GUISANTES SALTEADOS COM JAMON

Peas with Ham

Follow the recipe for Green Beans with Ham above, but use petits pois instead of green beans.

JUDIAS VERDES CON VINAGRETA

Green Beans with Vinaigrette

Judías verdes con vinagreta make an ideal winter salad, and as with other such vegetable salads, it is important to make sure the dressing is highly seasoned. If preferred, the beans may be marinated in the dressing for about an hour before serving.

1 lb green beans
1 tablespoon finely chopped scallions/spring onions
1 tablespoon finely chopped parsley
2 large ripe tomatoes
1 lemon
seasoning to taste

Vinaigrette:

1 tablespoon wine vinegar
4 tablespoons olive oil
seasoning to taste

Mix the vinaigrette by combining the vinegar, oil and seasoning and stirring well. Set aside.

Wash and trim the beans. Put the beans into a saucepan, cover with boiling water, add a little salt and cook for about 15-20 minutes over low heat until tender. When tender, drain; rinse in cold water and drain thoroughly.

Mix the beans with the chopped scallions and parsley and cover with vinaigrette sauce.

Garnish with sliced tomatoes and lemon wedges.

Serves 4.

LOMBARDA CON NARANJAS Y NUECES

Red Cabbage, Orange and Walnut Salad

The lively colors of this crunchy salad from Murcia brighten any winter day. It is particularly good served with game, rabbit and hot or cold ham.

1 small red cabbage
3 large oranges
3 stalks celery
10 walnuts—halved
2 tablespoons oil
1 tablespoon chopped parsley
1½ teaspoons paprika
seasoning to taste

Grate the rind of one orange and squeeze the juice. Set both aside.

Finely shred the cabbage leaves, discarding the core. Wash and trim the celery and chop into small pieces. Peel 2 oranges and separate into segments.

Mix together the orange segments, celery pieces, shredded cabbage and walnuts.

Make the dressing by combining the parsley, orange juice, rind, oil, seasoning and paprika. Pour the dressing over the salad and mix well.

Serves 4 to 6.

FRITURAS DE PATATAS CON BECHAMEL

Potato Fritters Filled with White Sauce

This is a simple but different way of serving potatoes. It is popular with adults and children alike.

6 medium potatoes
1 cup thick white sauce (see p. 206)
1½ cups fine breadcrumbs
2 beaten eggs
oil for frying

Peel and cut the potatoes into medium-thin slices. With a spatula spread a little of the white sauce over a slice of potato; put another potato slice on top (in sandwich form). Dip the potato sandwich into the beaten egg, then roll in breadcrumbs, coating generously. Continue in this manner until all the potatoes have been used.

Fry in hot oil until golden brown.

Serves 4 to 6.

PATATAS EN SALSA VERDE

Potatoes in Parsley Sauce

This is a rustic potato dish which is delicious as an accompaniment to poached cod or haddock. It can also be served separately as a substantial first course.

2 lbs potatoes
1 large onion—chopped
2 cloves garlic—chopped
3 tablespoons olive oil
1 cup peas
3 tablespoons chopped parsley
2 hard-boiled eggs—sliced
seasoning to taste
2 cups water

Peel and cut the potatoes into medium-thick slices.

Crush the chopped parsley in a mortar.

Put the oil in a large frying pan and sauté the onion until

soft. Add the parsley, garlic and potatoes; stir well and cook very gently for 10 minutes.

Then add the peas, season well and add the water. Cover and cook over low heat for about 15 minutes, until the potatoes are cooked.

Five minutes before serving, add the hard-boiled eggs and stir.

Serves 4.

PATATAS VIUDAS

Widowed Potatoes

This dish, with its rather unusual and striking title, is so called because the potatoes are normally served unaccompanied—as a soup—in the water in which they are cooked. However, drained of some of their liquid, *patatas viudas* are also a good accompaniment to roast or grilled meats. We prefer to eat them as a first course, served in individual soup dishes.

3 lbs potatoes
2 cloves garlic—chopped
1 large onion—chopped
1 teaspoon paprika
1 tablespoon chopped parsley
pinch powdered saffron
3 tablespoons olive oil
4 cups water
2 cups vegetable stock
seasoning to taste

Peel and cut the potatoes into medium-sized slices.

Put the oil into a large casserole, add the onions and garlic and sauté until soft. Then add the potatoe slices, water, stock, paprika, saffron and seasoning; stir well, cover with lid and cook for 25 minutes over low heat. Shake the pan occasionally during cooking.

When cooked, sprinkle with parsley and serve in individual soup plates.

Serves 6.

PERAS CON MAYONESA VERDE

Pears with Green Mayonnaise

This original dish makes a pleasant change served as the first course of a summer lunch or dinner. The slightly piquant filling contrasts well with the sweetness and flavor of the pears. We like to use the small green pears that are so plentiful in Spain in the summer. They are ideal for this recipe as they are firm but ripe, and they have a wonderful flavor.

4 sweet but firm eating pears

3 teaspoons lemon juice and 2 teaspoons olive oil for coating pears

Filling:

½ cup mayonnaise (see p. 208 or use prepared mayonnaise

1 egg white (large)

2 tablespoons minced scallions/spring onions

2 tablespoons finely chopped parsley

4 chopped anchovy fillets

1 teaspoon lime juice

1 level teaspoon mild tarragon-flavored mustard

Garnish:

12 lettuce leaves

12 stuffed olives

24 small cooked peeled shrimps/prawns (optional)

½ teaspoon paprika

To Make the Filling:

Whisk the egg white until stiff and set aside. Crush the parsley in a mortar, then transfer to a mixing bowl. Add the mayonnaise, scallions, anchovy fillets, lime juice and mustard, and mix well. Then fold in the stiff egg white and combine thoroughly.

Peel, half and core the pears, and coat with the oil and lemon juice combination to prevent discoloration.

Arrange a couple of lettuce leaves on each plate and place two pear halves on top. Fill the hollow centers of the pears with the mayonnaise mixture and place one stuffed olive and two shrimps (if used) on top of each half. Sprinkle with a little paprika and serve.

Serves 6.

PIMIENTOS ASADOS CON VINAGRETA

Roasted Red Peppers with Vinaigrette

This is a popular *tapa* (appetizer) dish, as well as being an excellent accompaniment to meat and fish.

3 large red peppers
vinaigrette sauce

Vinaigrette:

1 tablespoon wine vinegar
3 tablespoons olive oil
seasoning to taste

Mix the vinaigrette by combining the vinegar, oil and seasoning and stirring well. Set aside.

Wash and dry the red peppers. Place on a flameproof dish and cook in preheated, moderately hot oven for about 25-30 minutes, turning from time to time.

Remove the peppers from oven, place them on a large

plate and cover with another large plate or a cloth and allow to cool.

When cool, peel the peppers, cut in half, discard the seeds and cut the peppers into strips.

Before serving, pour over the vinaigrette sauce.

Serves 4.

PISTO

Stewed Vegetables

There are almost as many versions of *pisto* as there are people who make it; some omit the zucchini/courgettes or the eggplants/aubergines and, in some regions, the tomatoes are omitted. This is our version and we both love it as a first course.

1 large onion—chopped
3 cloves of garlic—chopped
1 large eggplant/aubergine—washed and diced
2 zucchini/courgettes—diced
2 green peppers—seeded and chopped
4 large ripe tomatoes—peeled and chopped
¼ cup olive oil
seasoning to taste
1 egg—lightly beaten

Put the oil into a large saucepan and sauté the onions, peppers and garlic until soft. Add the tomatoes, eggplant, zucchini and seasoning. Stir well. Cover and cook for a further 30-40 minutes.

Lower the heat and slowly add the beaten egg, stirring continuously. Remove from heat. Cover and allow to stand for a few minutes. Serve as starter or accompaniment to meat dishes.

Serves 6.

PUERROS CON JAMON Y BECHAMEL

Leeks with Ham in White Sauce

The delicately flavored, tender leeks combine wonderfully with salty cured ham and rich sauce. This dish makes a very tasty first course.

1 tablespoon oil
6-8 leeks
3 oz chopped *serrano* ham, or other cured ham
1 cup white sauce (see p. 206)
½ cup grated cheese—*manchego*, gruyere or similar

Clean the leeks by cutting in half lengthways, fanning open and washing under tap. Place the leeks in a large pan of boiling water and simmer until just tender (about 15 minutes). Drain and set aside.

Sauté the diced ham in the oil for a few minutes.

Arrange a layer of the leeks in a greased, ovenproof dish; sprinkle half the ham over the leeks and repeat with remaining leeks and ham. Pour the sauce over the top, sprinkle with cheese and bake in a preheated, moderately hot oven for 15 minutes.

Serves 4.

PUERROS GRATINADOS

Leeks Gratin

This simple leek dish is another typical example of the way vegetables are cooked in Spain. The leeks are simmered gently until tender and then combined with crispy bacon and cheese and baked until golden. Although this dish makes a very good accompaniment to cod, haddock and poultry, it is usually served as a separate course.

6-8 leeks
3 slices of smoked bacon—rind removed
¾ cup grated cheese—*manchego*, gruyere or similar
2 tablespoons butter
1 tablespoon oil
seasoning to taste

Clean the leeks by cutting in half lengthways and washing under tap. Place the leeks in a large pan of salted boiling water and simmer until just tender (about 15 minutes). Drain, place in a greased ovenproof dish and keep hot.

Cut the bacon into small pieces and sauté in the oil for a few minutes until golden. Spread the bacon over the leeks. Sprinkle with the cheese, freshly ground black pepper and dot with butter. Place in a preheated, moderately hot oven and cook until is golden brown (10-15 minutes).

Serves 4.

ARROZ

Rice Dishes

PAELLA

A romantic, but fanciful, story is often told about the origin of the word *paella*. This follows the line that one day a chef, who was very much in love with a beautiful young woman, created this elaborate dish especially *para ella*, which literally means "for her," and that, over time, the name *para ella* became shortened to *pa-ella*, now *paella*.

The truth, alas, is a little less romantic. *Paella*, in fact, takes its name from the large, shallow pan in which the dish is cooked and this is derived from the old French word for pan (*paele*, present-day *poêle*). In Spanish this large, round, flat pan is called a *paellera*. However, on a few occasions, when a *paellera* has not been available, we have used a large non-stick electric wok, which has given very good results. This, of course, would be considered a sacrilege by the purists, many of whom would never even dream of cooking a *paella* indoors. They believe, and with some justification, that nothing can compare with the taste of a *paella* cooked in the open air over a pine wood fire.

ARROZ

In Spain there are innumerable recipes for *paella*, from the very simple, and relatively inexpensive, to the most elaborate—almost every household has its own particular favorite. Some use chicken and pork, while others prefer to combine rabbit or veal with the fish. Again, the fish used varies according to availability and individual preference.

In fact, the dish's flexibility could well account for its popularity and certainly, outside Spain at least, *paella* seems to be considered as the country's national dish.

PAELLA A LA VALENCIANA

2 cups long grain rice
4-5 cups fish stock
¼ lb diced *chorizo*, or other garlic sausage
2 tablespoons diced cured ham
1 medium chicken—cut into a dozen pieces
3-4 squid—cleaned (see p. 94)
12 raw king prawns or lobster tails
2 cups (1 lb) peeled shrimps/prawns
2 cups mussels, or clams, or both—well-scrubbed (see p. 127)
freshly ground black pepper
1 large onion—chopped
1 large green pepper—chopped
3 cloves garlic—chopped
1 tablespoon chopped parsley
1 teaspoon paprika
½ teaspoon crushed saffron
1 bay leaf
½ cup olive oil
1 cup peas, fresh or frozen
2 teaspoons salt
2 lemons—cut into wedges
1 canned sweet red pepper

Put the oil in the *paellera* or large flat pan. Season the chicken pieces and sauté until light golden brown on both sides—sprinkle with paprika while cooking. Add the diced *chorizo* and ham, and continue cooking for another 5 minutes. Remove the meats from pan with a slotted spoon and set aside.

Add the uncooked lobster tails and/or king prawns in the shells to the pan and cook over high heat for about three minutes (turning the pieces occasionally), until the shells begin to turn pink. Then remove from pan and set aside.

In the same pan, cook the chopped onions, peppers, parsley and chopped garlic until soft (add a little more oil if necessary). Stir in saffron and add salt to taste. Now add the rice and mix well with the onion mixture. Add bay leaf, pour in stock and bring to boil. Lower heat immediately, and return the chicken, ham and sausage to the pan and cook the *paella*, uncovered, over a low heat for 15-20 minutes. After about ten minutes, add the squid (cut into medium-sized pieces), and a little more water, if necessary.

In the meantime, put the cleaned mussels and/or clams (use only those with closed shells) in a saucepan of boiling water, add salt to taste. As soon as the shells open, remove from heat. Drain, and discard that half of the shell which does not contain the mussel/clam. Set the mussels/clams aside.

Now add the peas to the *paella* and continue cooking for about 8-10 minutes. If necessary, add a little of the strained mussel/clam water. Finally, add the peeled shrimps, together with the previously cooked shellfish: lobster tails, king prawns, mussels, clams, and cook for further 5 minutes or so, until all the liquid has been absorbed and the rice is cooked but not too soft. Remove from heat, cover and allow to stand for 5 minutes. Before serving, decorate the *paella* with strips of the canned sweet red pepper and lemon wedges.

Serves 6.

Variations:

Omit chicken and use veal and/or pork.

Add white fish (hake, cod, monkfish) as well as the shellfish.

Omit peas and use French beans or artichoke hearts.

For how to clean squid see p. 94.
For how to clean mussels see p. 127.

ARROZ CON AZAFRAN

Saffron Rice

Saffron rice is extremely popular in Spain where it is often called *arroz de adorno*, which means rice served as an accompaniment, with *zarzuela de pescado* (fish stew), *riñones al jerez* (kidneys in sherry), as well as with shellfish, game and chicken.

Unfortunately, saffron is becoming rather expensive and increasingly nowadays yellow coloring is used as a substitute.

2 cups long-grain rice
4 cups boiling water
1 teaspoon salt (or to taste)
3 tablespoons olive oil
1 medium onion—chopped
a good pinch ground saffron, or substitute

Put the oil into a frying pan and sauté the onions until soft. Add the rice and stir until all the grains are coated with oil. Add the boiling water, salt, and the saffron. Cover and simmer gently until the rice is cooked and has absorbed all the liquid (around 20 minutes).

Fluff the rice with a fork. Transfer to a serving dish and keep warm.

Serves 4 to 6.

ARROZ BLANCO CON TOMATE

Boiled Rice with Tomato Sauce

Boiled rice with tomato sauce is a staple accompaniment to many dishes in Spain. It is excellent with ham, poultry, hard-boiled eggs and green beans.

2 cups long-grain rice
10 cups boiling water
2 teaspoons salt (or to taste)

Tomato Sauce:

3 tablespoons olive oil
3 cups canned chopped tomatoes (1 1/2 medium cans, or 24 oz)
1 large onion—finely chopped
½ teaspoon oregano
salt to taste
freshly ground black pepper
½ teaspoon sugar (optional)

Put the rice in large pan, add the boiling water and salt. Do not cover the pan, and cook vigorously until the rice is done (about 15 minutes). Then, drain off excess water, fluff rice with a fork and keep hot.

Meanwhile, put oil in large frying pan, add the chopped onion and sauté until soft. Add the canned tomatoes, salt, black pepper and oregano, and simmer for about 10 minutes. Pass the mixture through a fine sieve and add more salt and sugar, if desired.

Spoon the tomato sauce over the rice and serve immediately.

Serves 6.

ARROZ BLANCO CON TOMATE, CEBOLLA Y VINO BLANCO

Boiled Rice with Tomato, Onion and White Wine Sauce

This is a slightly more elaborate version of the previous recipe.

Ingredients are as *arroz blanco con tomate* plus:

2 tablespoons dry white wine
1 tablespoon chopped fresh parsley

Follow instructions for *arroz blanco con tomate,* but when adding tomatoes also add the wine and chopped parsley. Then continue as instructed.

Serves 6.

ARROZ BLANCO CON TOMATE Y JUDIAS VERDES

Boiled Rice with Green Beans and Tomato Sauce

This is a very economical dish and makes a good first course or light vegetarian supper.

As *arroz blanco con tomate* plus:

1 lb fresh green beans
1 clove garlic—chopped
¼ cup olive oil
salt to taste

Prepare *arroz blanco con tomate* as instructed in the recipe.

Top and tail beans. Then put them into a large pan and cover with boiling water. Add salt to taste and simmer gently for about 10-15 minutes until cooked. Then drain.

Meawhile, put the oil in a large frying pan, add the garlic

and sauté until golden. Add the drained beans and heat gently in the oil, stirring occasionally.

Place the hot rice in the middle of a large serving dish. Spoon the beans around the rice, then pour over the tomato sauce. Serve immediately

Serves 6.

ARROZ CON COLIFLOR Y CHORIZO

Rice with Cauliflower and Red Sausage

This has always been a favorite in our family. The almonds, chorizo and cauliflower combine very well with the rice to produce a delicious and inexpensive dish.

1 medium cauliflower—cooked
4 scallions/spring onions (or ½ onion)—chopped
1 leek—washed, dried and cut into pieces
1 clove garlic—chopped
3 cups boiled rice
2 tablespoons flaked toasted almonds
¼ cup oil
seasoning to taste
1 tablespoon fresh parsley
½ teaspoon paprika
pinch cumin
¼ lb piece *chorizo*, or other garlic sausage—sliced
2 tomatoes—sliced (for garnish)

In a large, shallow pan heat 3 tablespoons of oil and sauté the chopped scallions and garlic until soft. Stir in the *chorizo* slices. Break the cooked cauliflower into small pieces and add to the pan. Sauté for a couple of minutes or so. Then add the cooked rice and seasoning. Mix well and continue cooking over a low heat for 2-3 minutes. Add the chopped parsley, paprika, cumin and toasted almonds and mix thoroughly. Cook for an additional 5 minutes, stirring occasionaly.

Either transfer the cauliflower and rice onto a heated serving dish, or serve directly on individual plates and garnish with sliced tomatoes.

Serves 4-6.

ARROZ CON POLLO

Rice with Chicken

Arroz con pollo is a dish which is typical of almost every region of Spain. The rice is cooked in the same pan with the chicken and vegetables and the result is an extremely succulent and tasty dish.

1 medium chicken—cut into serving pieces
1 onion—chopped
1 green pepper—chopped
3 medium ripe tomatoes—peeled and chopped
1 clove garlic—chopped
1 tablespoon parsley—finely chopped
good pinch each of ground saffron, cumin, paprika
½ teaspoon oregano
¼ cup oil
2 tablespoons chopped cured ham (about 1 oz)
1 cup long-grain rice
2 cups water
salt to taste
2 teaspoons lemon juice

Crush the garlic and parsley in a mortar, add the saffron, oregano and salt to taste. Stir in the lemon juice, one tablespoon oil and mix well. Coat the chicken pieces with this mixture and allow to stand for about 30-40 minutes.

Heat the remaining oil in a large, shallow pan and brown

the chicken quickly over moderately hot heat. Transfer the chicken to a plate. Add the chopped onion and pepper to the pan and sauté until soft. Stir in the tomatoes and ham. Add the rice and mix well to coat in the oil. Stir in the cumin, paprika and salt to taste and add the water. Mix thoroughly and then return the chicken pieces to the pan. Cover and allow to simmer gently for about 25 minutes, until all the water has been absorbed and the chicken is tender.

Serves 4.

CIGALAS EMBORACHADAS CON ARROZ

Drunken Scampi with Rice

This innovative, exuberant recipe is a splendid dinner party dish. It makes a very appealing first course and is also suitable for a light main course.

1½ cups good quality long-grain rice
7 cups water
2 teaspoons salt (or to taste)
1 clove garlic (optional)—chopped
½ cup (about 4 oz) chicken—diced
¼ cup (about 2 oz) cured ham—chopped
16-20 raw scampi tails or king prawns
16-20 large, ripe, white grapes—halved and seeded
1 large onion—chopped
1 green pepper—chopped
2 zucchini/courgettes—chopped
1 teaspoon dried mixed herbs
1 cup red wine
¼ cup water
½ cup oil
seasoning to taste
freshly ground black pepper

Put the rice into a large saucepan with the water and salt. Bring to the boil and cook vigorously (uncovered) until rice is done (about 15 minutes). Then strain off excess water and fluff rice with a fork.

Meanwhile, place the scampi in a dish and pour over the wine. Let marinate.

Put 4 tablespoons of oil into a large frying pan and sauté the chopped onion and pepper until soft. Then add the diced chicken, ham and zucchini, cover and continue cooking gently for around 15 minutes. Now add the scampi, wine, grapes, water and seasoning to taste to the vegetables and chicken in the pan. Cover and simmer for 5 minutes, until the scampi is cooked.

While the scampi is cooking, put the rest of the oil into another frying pan and, if garlic is used, lightly sauté until golden. Add the boiled rice and fry for a few minutes, stirring occasionally, until rice is well coated and completely heated through.

Place the rice on a serving dish and spoon over the "drunken" scampi, chicken and vegetable mixture; sprinkle with ground black pepper and serve immediately.

Serves 4 to 6 as a first course.

ENSALADA DE ARROZ VALENCIANA

Valencian Rice Salad

This is a refreshing, tangy rice salad from the Levante region of eastern Spain. It makes an excellent first course or supper dish.

3 cups boiled rice
1 large orange—peeled and sliced
½ green pepper—chopped
1 canned sweet red pepper—sliced
2 large tomatoes—quartered

3-4 hard-boiled eggs
1 small can artichoke hearts (8 oz size approx.)
1 medium can asparagus (16 oz size approx.)
vinaigrette (see p. 215)
chopped parsley to garnish

Mix together the rice and green peppers and add two tablespoons of vinaigrette sauce, mix thoroughly. Press the rice into a round mold and put in the refrigerator for one hour.

Then gently remove rice from mold and place in a mound in the middle of a large platter. Arrange the tomatoes, eggs, orange slices and drained artichoke hearts around the base of the rice. Place the drained asparagus spears vertically against the rice mound and decorate with the sliced sweet red peppers and chopped parsley.

Serve with vinaigrette sauce.

Serves 6.

Variation:

The "crown" of asparagus spears may be alternated with king prawns.

ENSALADA SENCILLA DE ARROZ Y ATUN

Simple Rice and Tuna Salad

A simple, straightforward winter or summer salad, which is equally good for a light lunch or supper dish.

3 cups boiled rice
1 can light tuna (approx. 10 oz size)
1 green pepper—chopped
3 ripe tomatoes—chopped
1 cup cooked green beans—chopped
vinaigrette (see p. 215)
seasoning to taste

Flake the tuna with a fork (retaining the oil). Combine the vegetables and rice and then add the flaked tuna, oil and seasoning to taste and mix well. Chill for one hour and serve with vinaigrette sauce.

Serves 6.

HOW TO CLEAN SQUID

1)Pull the body section of squid away from the head and tentacles.

2)Take the head section and, with a sharp knife or scissors, cut off the tentacles just above the eyes. Discard the eye section. Keep the tentacles, and chop if recipe so requires.

3)Take the cone-shaped body section and remove the stiff pen or quill and the entrails (the white, liquidy material). Discard pen and entrails, but keep the grey-blue ink sac found in the inner part of the body section—if your recipe requires this.

Keep the empty cone-shaped body section.

4)Peel away the thin purple skin or membrane which covers the body section. Then turn the cone-shaped body section inside out and wash well.

5)The squid is now ready for use.

HUEVOS

Egg Dishes

HUEVOS A LA FLAMENCA

Baked Eggs with Vegetables, Ham and Sausage

This is a very old and popular dish in Spain. The thick *sofrito* sauce, made with lightly fried vegetables and meats, forms a base or bed on which the colorful eggs, peas, asparagus and sweet red pepper strips rest. The dish is then baked in a moderate oven until the eggs have set.

Sofrito:

1 green pepper—seeded and chopped

1 medium onion—chopped

2 cloves garlic—chopped

2 medium ripe tomatoes—peeled and chopped or 6 tablespoons canned chopped tomatoes)

2 tablespoons (about 1 oz) chopped *serrano,* or other cured ham

1 *chorizo,* or other garlic sausage (approx. 3 oz)—sliced

1 tablespoon chopped parsley

1 bay leaf

3-4 tablespoons olive oil
3 tablespoons water
seasoning to taste

Eggs and Vegetables:
4-8 eggs (1 or 2 eggs per person)
4 tablespoons cooked peas
4-8 asparagus spears—cooked
1 canned sweet red pepper—drained and cut into strips
seasoning to taste
parsley to garnish

Make the *Sofrito*:

Put the oil into a large, shallow pan and sauté the onions, garlic and green peppers until soft. Add the chopped cured ham and *chorizo* slices, stir well and continue cooking for 2-3 minutes.

Stir in the tomatoes, water, bay leaf, parsley and seasoning and simmer until most of the liquid has been absorbed. Discard the bay leaf.

Spoon the *sofrito* into a greased, ovenproof dish, large enough to hold the sauce, eggs and vegetables.

Then prepare the eggs:

Break the eggs and arrange them one at a time on top of the *sofrito*. Decorate with the peas, asparagus and strips of red peppers. Season the eggs to taste.

Place in a preheated, moderately hot oven for around 8 minutes, or until the eggs are just set.

Garnish with fresh parsley and serve immediately with crusty bread.

Serves 4.

HUEVOS DUROS CON BECHAMEL

Hard-Boiled Eggs with White Sauce

This simple dish is another traditional stand-by as the first course of a family lunch or as a light evening meal.

6 hard-boiled eggs
1 tablespoon chopped parsley
3 slices bacon—chopped
few drops lemon juice
seasoning to taste
1 tablespoon oil
1 cup white sauce (see p. 67)
½ cup grated cheese

Sauté the chopped bacon in the oil for 2 minutes and stir in the chopped parsley. Set aside.

Cut the eggs in half lengthways and remove the yolks. Put the yolks into a bowl and mash with the back of a spoon. Add the chopped bacon, parsley, lemon juice, seasoning to taste and one tablespoon of the white sauce. Mix thoroughly. Refill the egg whites with the mixture and put the stuffed eggs into an ovenproof dish. Cover with the white sauce and sprinkle with grated cheese.

Place in a preheated, moderately hot oven for about 10 minutes, until lightly golden.

Serves 6 as a first course.

HUEVOS DUROS MIMOSAS

Hard-Boiled Eggs Mimosa

This is a very attractive and tasty dish. It is so called because of the mimosa effect made by grating the egg yolk on top of the white mayonnaise.

6 hard-boiled eggs
3 small anchovy fillets—chopped
ground black pepper
salt to taste
1 generous cup mayonnaise (see p. 208)

To garnish:
3 tomatoes—sliced
lettuce leaves
sprigs watercress

Cut the eggs in half lengthways and remove the yolks. Reserve 2 yolks.

Put 4 yolks into a bowl and mash with the back of a spoon; add the chopped anchovies, salt to taste and ground pepper and mix. Stir in one tablespoon of the mayonnaise and mix thoroughly. Refill the egg whites with the mixture.

Line a serving dish with the lettuce leaves and place the stuffed eggs on top (filling side down). Cover the eggs with the rest of the mayonnaise, and grate the 2 reserved egg yolks over the mayonnaise.

Garnish with sliced tomatoes and watercress.

Serves 6 as a first course.

HUEVOS FRITOS
Fried Eggs

Huevos fritos are delicious served with fried rice and tomato sauce. They are also an integral part of the well-known dish *huevos a la cubana* (Cuban-style fried eggs), which consists of fried eggs, rice and lightly fried bananas. Again, Spanish-style fried eggs are the crowning glory of *huevos a la valenciana,* in which a mixture of fried onions, tomatoes, peppers, raisins and ground almonds is stirred into freshly boiled rice; fried bananas are then added and the whole thing is topped with fried eggs.

8 eggs
1 cup oil for frying
seasoning to taste

The eggs are usually fried two at a time.

Pour the oil into a medium-sized, shallow frying pan and heat. Reduce the heat to moderate, break the eggs and add them two at a time to the oil. With a spatula gently fold the egg whites over the yolks so that the yolks are completely hidden. Allow to cook for about a minute, until the whites have set. Then remove the eggs from the pan, drain, season and serve immediately.

Serves 4.

FRITURAS DE HUEVOS RELLENOS, CON SALSA DE TOMATE

Fried Stuffed Eggs, with Tomato Sauce

This colorful and original dish makes an excellent first course or *tapa* (appetizer), and can form the basis of a light supper dish, served with crusty bread and salad.

4 hard-boilded eggs
½ cup mushrooms—finely chopped
¼ cup (about 2 oz) finely chopped *serrano*, or other cured ham
1 tablespoon chopped parsley
2 tablespoons oil
seasoning to taste
½ cup thick white sauce (see p. 206)
2 eggs—well beaten
1 cup dry breadcrumbs
tomato sauce (see p. 212)
oil for deep frying

Make the sauces as indicated on the relevant pages. Set aside.

Cut the hard-boilded eggs in half lengthwise. Remove the yolks and grate into a bowl, then set aside.

Sauté the chopped mushrooms in 2 tablespoons of oil until soft, add the chopped ham and parsley, and continue cooking for another 2-3 minutes. Add the grated egg yolks, stir in the white sauce, season to taste and mix well. Allow to cool.

Reshape each egg white half in the form of a whole egg by filling it with stuffing and mounding up to the shape of a whole egg.

Coat the egg shapes with beaten egg and cover generously with breadcrumbs. Fry the eggs in deep, hot oil until golden brown. Meanwhile, reheat the tomato sauce.

Serve the eggs immediately with hot tomato sauce.

Serves 4.

HUEVOS NEVADOS AL PLATO CON QUESO Y JAMON

Baked Snow Eggs with Grated Cheese and Ham

This attractive and mouthwatering dish seems to delight everyone. It makes an ideal light supper, and it is always a pleasure to see just how much family and friends enjoy such a simple but original dish.

4 whole eggs
2 egg whites
½ cup grated cheese
¼ cup (about 2 oz) *serrano*, or other cured ham—finely chopped
1½ tablespoon butter
4 teaspoons light cream

1 tablespoon oil
seasoning to taste

Put the egg whites in a bowl. Separate the yolks and whites of the four whole eggs. Add the 4 egg whites to the other 2 in the bowl. Whisk the egg whites until stiff, then gently fold in half the grated cheese. Melt the butter in a earthenware dish and extend it over the bottom. Spoon the beaten egg whites into the dish and spread evenly.

Make four shallow nests in the egg white and put one yolk into each. Season to taste, add one teaspoon of cream to the top of each yolk and sprinkle the remaining cheese over the beaten egg whites. Put into a preheated, hot oven immediately and cook for about 8 minutes, or until the egg white turns lightly golden and the yolks are just set.

Meanwhile, sauté the chopped ham in the oil for 2-3 minutes.

Remove the eggs from the oven, sprinkle with the chopped ham and serve immediately.

Serves 4.

Variations:

Instead of chopped ham, use chopped sautéed mushrooms, asparagus tips, or chopped anchovies.

PIPERRADA

Scrambled Eggs, Peppers and Tomatoes

Piperrada is a tasty dish from the Basque region of Spain. It makes a very pleasant light lunch or supper.

2 sweet red peppers—seeded and chopped
1 green pepper—seeded and chopped
1 large onion—chopped
3 medium-sized ripe tomatoes—peeled and chopped
(or one 8 oz can chopped tomatoes)

6 tablespoons oil
8 wafer-thin slices of *serrano*, or other cured ham
6 eggs—beaten
4 slices toast or fried bread
seasoning to taste

Put 5 tablespoons of oil into a large, shallow pan and sauté the onions and peppers until soft. Stir in the tomatoes and season to taste. Allow to cook gently for about 10 minutes.

Meanwhile, put the remaining tablespoon of oil into another pan and sauté the ham for about a minute (add a little more oil if required).

Pour the beaten eggs into the vegetable mixture and cook, stirring gently, until the eggs are just set. Top with the ham and serve immediately with toast or fried bread.

Serves 4.

TORTILLA DE PATATAS

Tortilla de patatas, Spanish potato omelet, is perhaps the most well-known of all Spanish dishes. It is extremely versatile, lending itself to many different variations according to individual taste: some people like to serve it with mayonnaise or hot tomato sauce; some like to add more onion, while others prefer to omit the onion completely; many like a more elaborate version and combine the potatoes with other fillings such as ham, *chorizo*, tuna, prawns, or a variety of vegetables. It can be served hot or cold, though in Spain it is the cold potato omelet which is the most popular. *Tortilla de patatas* is equally good as a first course, as the main course of a light lunch or supper, and as a *tapa*, in which case it is usually served cut into small squares or wedges.

TORTILLA DE PATATAS
Spanish Potato Omelet

2 lbs potatoes—peeled and diced
4 large eggs
1 tablespoon chopped onion
salt to taste
1 cup oil

Heat the oil in a heavy frying pan. Add the potatoes and salt and cook for about 5 minutes. Add the onion and continue cooking until the potatoes are just soft, but not brown. Remove the vegetables from the oil and drain well.

Beat the eggs in a large bowl, season to taste and stir in the cooked potatoes and onions.

Put 3 tablespoons of oil into a medium-sized, non-stick frying pan and heat; pour in the egg and potato mixture. Spread it evenly in the pan and cook over a moderate heat for 2-3 minutes, shaking the pan occasionally. When the bottom of the omelet is firm, take a large plate or flat frying pan lid (we prefer the latter), cover the pan and then carefully invert the pan so that the omelet is turned out onto the plate/lid. Then slide the omelet back into the pan and cook the other side until golden brown. If the top of the omelette is not golden brown, repeat the inversion process and cook the omelet for another minute or so to give a golden brown appearance to both sides.

Serves 4 as a main course. Often accompanied by a mixed salad.

TORTILLA DE PATATAS Y ESPARRAGOS
Potato and Asparagus Omelet

Use equal quantities of potatoes and fresh asparagus. Prepare the potatoes as before. Wash the asparagus, cut off the tough end parts and dice. Cook the potatoes in the oil for

5 minutes and then add the asparagus pieces. Fry gently until the vegetables are tender. Then proceed as for potato omelet.

TORTILLA DE PATATAS, PIMIENTO Y CHORIZO

Potato, Pepper and Chorizo Omelet

Use the same ingredients as for potato omelet, plus half a green pepper (chopped) and ¼ cup (about 2 oz) diced *chorizo* or other garlic sausage.

Prepare the potatoes and onions as indicated in the recipe for potato omelet, adding the chopped pepper at the same time as the onion, and fry until the vegetables are tender. Sauté the diced *chorizo* for a couple of minutes in a little oil, then combine with the drained potatoes, onions and peppers. Proceed as for potato omelet.

TORTILLA DE PATATAS Y ATUN

Potato and Tuna Omelet

Use the same ingredients as for potato omelet, plus a small can (3 oz size approx.) of tuna, drained and flaked. The tuna should be mixed with the cooked and drained potatoes and onions. Then proceed as for potato omelet.

PESCADOS Y MARISCOS

Fish and Shellfish

ATUN ENCEBOLLADO

"Onioned" Tuna

Atún encebollado is particularly popular in the Cadiz region of southern Spain, where fresh tuna is plentiful. If fresh tuna is not available, swordfish or baby shark are good substitutes—both as far as the texture of the fish and the combination of flavors are concerned. The dish could not be easier to prepare, and it lends itself to many variations.

2 lbs fresh tuna steaks (skin removed)
3 onions—peeled and chopped
¼ cup olive oil

bay leaf
1 tablespoon chopped parsley
1 teaspoon all-purpose flour
¾ cup white wine
seasoning to taste

Pour the oil into large flameproof casserole or frying pan and sauté the onion until soft; then stir in flour and mix well. Pour in the wine, stir, and bring to the boil. Reduce heat immediately and place the fish in pan. Add parsley, bay leaf and seasoning to taste. Cover with lid and cook over low heat for about 30 minutes, stirring occasionally (add a little water if necessary).

Serve with saffron rice or boiled potatoes.

Serves 4.

Variation:

Tomatoes are often included in this dish—about 3 medium-sized ripe tomatoes, peeled and chopped should be added after mixing in the flour. (If sweet tomatoes are not available, use 4 tablespoons of canned chopped tomatoes.) Then proceed as above.

PASTEL DE ATUN

Tuna Pie

This is a tasty and inexpensive recipe which makes a hearty lunch or supper dish. We like to serve it with parsley potatoes and French beans.

10 oz canned tuna in oil
1 large green pepper—chopped
2 large onions—chopped
1 tablespoon tomato paste/purée
1 tablespoon fresh parsley—chopped
½ teaspoon dried mixed herbs

4-5 tablespoons sunflower oil (or other light oil)
seasoning to taste
10 oz puff pastry

Open tuna and drain off excess oil. Put the oil into a large, shallow pan and sauté the chopped onions and peppers until soft, add parsley and herbs and cook for additional 2 minutes. Season to taste, add the tomato paste and flaked tuna, and mix well.

Roll out pastry and cover the bottom of a greased 8 inch (approx.) pie dish with half of the pastry. Cover with foil, weigh down with uncooked rice and bake blind for 10 minutes in a moderate oven. Then remove the foil and fill the pastry case with the tuna and onion filling. Cover with the remaining pastry. Brush pastry with beaten egg yolk and place the pie in preheated, moderate oven for 30 minutes, until golden brown.

Serves 4.

FIESTA DE ATUN

Tuna Fish Fiesta

This is a very flexible and colorful dish suitable for a substantial lunch or dinner. It lends itself to many variations and has the advantage that it can be prepared in advance to the point of covering with the white sauce. All that is then required is that it be placed in the oven and cooked for 20 minutes before serving.

10 oz canned tuna in oil
4-5 medium-sized boiled (but firm) potatoes—sliced
½ cooked cauliflower (medium)
1 cup cooked rice
6 tablespoons canned chopped tomatoes
1 tablespoon tomato paste/purée

2 onions—chopped
2 cups white sauce (see p. 206)
seasoning to taste
½ teaspoon dried mixed herbs
3-4 tablespoons olive oil

Sauté the chopped onions in the olive oil until soft and add seasoning to taste.

Cover the bottom of a large (not too shallow) greased pie dish with the sliced cooked potatoes—use all the potatoes. Combine the canned tomatoes with the tomato paste, mixed herbs and seasoning, then spoon half the mixture over the potatoes.

Mix the cooked rice with the cauliflower florets and spread evenly over the previous layer. Cover with the remaining tomato mixture.

Open tuna and pour off excess oil. Flake the tuna and mix with the fried onions, then spread this mixture over previous layer in the dish. Finally, cover the whole thing with white sauce and place in a preheated, moderately hot oven for 20 minutes. Serve immediately.

Serves 4.

MANJAR DE ATUN Y AGUACATE

Tuna and Avocado Mousse

Manjar is a beautiful old Spanish word meaning an exquisite or delightful dish, and this tuna and avocado mousse is indeed a delight both to behold and to eat. Its attractive shape, pale green coloring and bright garnishes make it a real success with everyone. We often serve it with *patatas aliñadas* (potatoes in vinaigrette sauce) and crusty bread.

10 oz fresh tuna (or canned light tuna in oil)
2 ripe avocados

1 pkg (1 tablespoon) natural gelatin
seasoning to taste
1 teaspoon anchovy extract/essence
green food coloring
2 egg whites
¼ cup light cream
1 lemon
1 tablespoon dry *fino* sherry (optional)

For the Garnish:

A few sprigs of parsley, 2 cups diced cucumber, 1 small canned sweet red pepper (cut into strips), a few toasted flaked almonds and one black olive

Poach the fresh tuna in one cup of water with 1 teaspoon of lemon juice and seasoning until tender. Drain, remove bones and skin. (If canned tuna is used drain off some of the oil.) Then flake the fish with a fork. Peel and stone the avocados and cut into small pieces. Put the avocado pieces, anchovy extract, tuna, sherry, a few drops of lemon juice and seasoning into a large bowl and mash with a potato masher or fork, then beat until smooth (or blend in a food processor). Dissolve the gelatine in ¼ cup of hot water. Whisk the egg whites until stiff.

Add the dissolved gelatin to the avocado and tuna mixture. Then stir in the cream and add a few drops of green food coloring. When well mixed, fold in the beaten egg white. Put the whole mixture into a fish mold. Place in the refrigerator, and allow to set for 2-3 hours.

When ready, turn out onto a serving dish. Cut the black olive in half and place on the top (head) part of the fish mousse to make the eyes. Cut a canned sweet red pepper into strips and place at the bottom of fish to make fins. Garnish with fresh parsley, flaked almonds and cucumber.

Serves 4.

BACALAO EN SAL AL HORNO
Cod Baked in Salt

This is a very original Spanish recipe whereby the cod is covered in a crust of salt which allows the fish to cook in its own juices. The result is a succulent, firm and delicately flavored fish. We like to serve it with something slightly piquant such as *remolachas aliñadas, con ajo* (fresh beets/beetroot in garlic vinaigrette dressing) and green mayonnaise.

2 lb tail piece cod (on the bone and with skin)
2 lb salt

(For *bacalao en sal* the amount of salt used should equal the weight of the fish. The salt will bake into a crust and this is easily removed when the fish is cooked. This same salt may be used more than once.)

Wash fish and dry on paper towel. The thick (cut) end of the fish should be covered with foil.

Place half the salt in a layer on the bottom of a large ovenproof dish. Put the fish on top of salt and press well in. Cover top of fish with remaining salt.

Place in preheated, moderate oven and cook for 40-45 minutes. Check occasionally that the salt has not become dislodged. If so, take a palette knife or large spoon and replace it. The salt will bake into a firm crust.

When cooked lift off the salt, removing the skin of the fish at the same time.

Serves 3-4.

Green Mayonnaise:

Crush 1 tablespoon chopped parsley in a mortar. Add two tablespoons of mayonnaise and mix well. Add a few chopped capers, diced cucumber and stir in a couple of drops of green food coloring.

BACALAO A LA VIZCAINA
Cod Basque Style

Vizcaya is one of the Basque Country's three provinces and its capital city is Bilbao. The Basque Country is famed for its gastronomy and its fish dishes in particular. Many Basques believe that the fish caught in their bay, especially cod, is incomparably better than that from the coastal waters of other parts of Spain. We have been served this delicious cod dish many times on visits to Bilbao and can bear witness to the freshness and quality of Basque cuisine.

1½-2 lbs cod steaks (1 large or 2 small per person)
1 large onion—chopped
3 ripe tomatoes—peeled and chopped
(or 4 tablespoons canned chopped tomatoes)
1 sweet red pepper—chopped
1 tablespoon chopped *serrano*, or other cured ham
2 tablespoons fried breadcrumbs
1 teaspoon finely grated unsweetened chocolate
2 cloves garlic—chopped
2 hard-boiled egg yolks—grated
3 tablespoons olive oil
seasoning to taste
½ cup water

Put the oil into a large frying pan and sauté the onion and garlic until soft. Add the chopped pepper, tomatoes, fried breadcrumbs, egg yolks, chocolate, ham and water, and stir well. Allow to cook for about 5 minutes (adding a little more water if necessary). Place half of the sauce on the bottom of an ovenproof dish and place fish on top. Spoon the remaining sauce over the fish. Cover with a lid or foil, place in preheated, moderately hot oven and cook for 25-30 minutes. Half way through cooking time, remove the lid or foil and cook uncovered for the remainder.

Serves 4.

BACALAO EN SALSA VERDE

Cod in Parsley Sauce

This simple dish is equally good with any firm-textured white fish.

4 good-sized cod (or hake) steaks
½ cup white wine
1 cup water or fish stock
1 onion—chopped
2½ tablespoons chopped fresh parsley
1½ tablespoons all-purpose flour
1 clove garlic
bay leaf
4 tablespoons olive oil
seasoning to taste
flour for coating fish

Roll fish in seasoned flour and sauté in the oil for a couple of minutes on each side. Remove fish and drain on paper towel.

Sauté the garlic clove in the oil until soft. Remove it and put the garlic clove in a mortar together with the salt and chopped parsley, and crush to a paste.

Put the chopped onion into the pan which contains the oil, and sauté until soft. Add 1½ tablespoons of flour and mix well. Stir in the parsley paste, then add the wine and water/fish stock, stirring continuously. Season to taste and when the sauce begins to thicken, reduce heat and add the fish steaks. Cover and simmer gently for about 15 minutes over moderately low heat until the fish is cooked.

Serves 4.

BACALAO CON TOMATES
Salt Cod with Tomatoes

This typical salt cod dish is popular all over Spain. It is also very good with smoked haddock.

1¼ lbs salt cod
5 potatoes
2 large onions—sliced
4 medium-sized ripe tomatoes—peeled and chopped
3 cloves garlic—chopped
1 large sweet red pepper—cut into strips
4 tablespoons olive oil
parsley to garnish
seasoning to taste

Cut fish into pieces. Remove salt by soaking in water for at least 24 hours, changing the water occasionally. Afterwards remove fish and drain. Peel and boil potatoes until just cooked. Drain and cut into slices. Rinse the cod pieces and place in saucepan of boiling water (enough water to cover fish). Simmer for 12-15 minutes, until fish is tender and flaky.

Remove from heat and drain. Prepare fish by removing bones and skin and separating into rough flakes.

Slice the onions and sauté in the oil for 5 minutes. Add the chopped tomatoes and red peppers (cut into strips), garlic and seasoning, then sauté for a further 5 minutes until mixture is soft.

Grease a casserole dish and cover the bottom with the sliced potatoes (reserving same amount). Place the fish on top of the potatoes and cover with remaining potatoes. Spoon the onion, tomato and sweet red pepper mixture on top. Place in center of preheated, moderate oven and cook for 20-25 minutes. Garnish with parsley and serve.

Serves 4 to 6.

BESUGO AL HORNO

Baked Bream (or Red Snapper)

A beautifully simple, but delicious way of cooking this succulent white fish in which lemon wedges are inserted into the flesh. It is ideal for a light summer lunch, served with sautéed tomatoes and baked red peppers in vinaigrette.

1 large sea bream (about 3 lbs)—cleaned
2 tablespoons butter
¾ cup white wine
2 lemons
1 tablespoon fresh parsley—chopped
seasoning to taste
bay leaf

Sprinkle fish with salt (both sides) and set aside for 30 minutes.

Then wash off salt and dry the fish on a paper towel.

Place the fish in a large, well greased, ovenproof dish. Cut one lemon into thin wedges. Make two or three incisions in the flesh of the fish, and insert a lemon wedge into each. Pour the wine over the fish and dot with the butter. Sprinkle with parsley, a few drops of lemon juice, seasoning and add a bay leaf.

Cover with foil and place in preheated, moderately hot oven for approximately 30 minutes. Then remove the foil and cook for a further 10 minutes, until tender. Serve immediately

Serves 4.

BESUGO EN SIDRA
Bream (or Red Snapper) in Cider

This recipe is similar to *mero al oloroso,* but cider is used instead of sherry.

1½-2 lbs skinned bream or snapper slices
1 medium onion—chopped
1 bay leaf
seasoning to taste
1 cup cider
½ cup water
1 tablespoon all-purpose flour
1 tablespoon butter
1 tablespoon parsley—chopped
¼ cup light cream

Put the fish slices into a shallow pan with onions, bay leaf, seasoning, cider and water. Poach for approximatley 20 minutes, until tender.

Then remove fish from the pan and drain. Strain the poaching liquid through a fine sieve and reserve.

Melt the butter in another pan and stir in flour to form a paste or roux. Gradually add the strained poaching liquid, stirring continuously and simmer gently until a light creamy consistency is reached. Stir in the cream and chopped parsley and mix well. Check for seasoning.

Put fish back into pan and heat through for a few minutes in the sauce. Serve immediately.

Serves 4.

CABALLAS RELLENAS DE MANZANAS Y PASAS
Mackerel Stuffed with Apples and Sultanas

During the summer months in Spain mackerel is often barbecued, together with sardines, and eaten outdoors.

Most people believe that this is by far the best way to eat these juicy fish. However, the following recipe makes a pleasant change and the tart flavor of the apples combines well with the mackerel's rich juices.

6 medium mackerel
2 medium tart apples—peeled, cored and chopped
1 tablespoon sultanas/golden raisins
1 medium onion—chopped
rind of 1 lime
3 tablespoons *migas* (see p. 50)
seasoning to taste
3 tablespoons oil
1 tablespoon fresh tarragon—chopped

Wash, slit open and clean the mackerel, and cut off heads.

Put the oil into a large frying pan and sauté the apples and onions until soft. Stir in the lime rind, *migas*, sultanas and seasoning to taste. Mix well, then divide the mixture into six equal portions and stuff the fish. Secure with small skewers or cocktail sticks.

Place the fish on a greased, ovenproof dish and put into a preheated, moderately hot oven for about 30-35 minutes, until cooked.

Remove from oven, sprinkle with chopped tarragon and serve immediately.

Serves 6.

CALAMARES CON PUERROS—*DE ABUELA*

Granny's Squid with Leeks

The combination of squid and leeks is particularly good, especially when enhanced by the addition of a little *fino* sherry. As the title indicates, the dish has been a firm family favorite for years.

1½ lb squid
2 medium leeks
1 large sweet red pepper—chopped
2 medium zucchini/courgettes
3 carrots—peeled and cut into medium pieces
3 cloves garlic
2 sprigs of tarragon—chopped
1 tablespoon parsley—chopped
2 tablespoons *fino* (dry) sherry
1 bay leaf
¼ cup olive oil
seasoning to taste

Clean the squid as indicated on p. 94, then cut into small rings or pieces and set aside.

Clean the leeks and cut into rings.

Place the oil in a large frying pan with the chopped garlic, bay leaf, herbs and seasoning to taste. Sauté for few minutes until garlic is soft. Add the leeks, carrots and chopped red peppers, and cook for a few minutes.

Meanwhile, top and tail the zucchini and slice into rings. Add to the pan, stirring well, and cook for 5 minutes over medium heat. Then add the squid and sherry (add a little water if necessary). Mix thoroughly, check seasoning, cover and cook gently for about 20-25 minutes.

Care should be taken not to over-cook the squid.

Serve on a bed of rice.

Serves 4 to 5.

SORPRESA DE CALAMARES

Squid Surprise

Easy to prepare and simple to cook.

1 lb squid

2 medium onions—chopped
2 large ripe tomatoes—chopped
1 green pepper—chopped
2 cloves garlic—chopped
1½ cups chopped mushrooms
1 cup peeled shrimps/prawns (about 8 oz)
½ teaspoon mixed herbs
2-3 tablespoons olive oil
¼ cup white wine
seasoning to taste

Wash and clean squid thoroughly then chop into pieces.

Chop the onions, pepper and garlic. Then put these into a large, shallow pan, together with the olive oil, and sauté until soft. Add the chopped mushrooms, tomatoes, squid, herbs and seasoning, mix well, cover and cook for about 15 minutes. Pour in the wine and add the shrimps, stir well and cook for a further 10-15 minutes.

Serve with saffron rice and green beans.

Serves 4.

CALAMARES EN SU TINTA

Squid in Its Own Ink Sauce

This is another simple way of cooking squid. The dark blue-black, distinctive sauce makes this dish particularly interesting and we like to serve it with rice and small fried green peppers.

2 lbs squid
1 large onion—chopped
2 cloves garlic—finely chopped
1 tablespoon fresh parsley—chopped
¼ cup olive oil
pinch nutmeg

seasoning to taste
1 tablespoon all-purpose flour
½ cup water
½ cup white wine
1 teaspoon cornstarch/corn flour

Clean squid thoroughly (see p. 94), reserving the ink sacs. Cut the squid into pieces.

Heat the olive oil in a large pan and add the onions, garlic and parsley and cook for a couple of minutes. Then add the squid, nutmeg and seasoning and cook over a moderate heat for about 15 minutes.

Put the ink sacs in a sieve and break open with a spoon or fork, squeezing out the ink. Discard the sacs. Mix the cornstarch with a little water and add to the ink, together with the remaining water and the wine.

Stir the ink mixture into the squid, cover and cook for an additional 15 minutes or so, until the squid is tender.

Serves 4-6

CAZON CON TOMATE

Tope (Baby Shark) with Tomatoes

This recipe is from the Cádiz region of southern Spain where *cazón* is plentiful. It is important that the shark used in this recipe is the more tender baby shark. We like to serve this with sautéed potatoes and green beans.

4 large (8 small) tope steaks
3 tablespoons *fino* dry sherry
1 medium onion—chopped
2 cloves garlic—chopped
½ teaspoon mixed herbs
3 tablespoons olive oil
1½ lbs ripe tomatoes—skinned and chopped
1 teaspoon all-purpose flour

2 tablespoons fresh breadcrumbs
1 bay leaf
seasoning to taste
parsley to garnish

Place the tope in a greased, ovenproof dish and pour the sherry over. Cover and leave for about 2 hours, turning from time to time.

Meanwhile, put the oil into a saucepan and fry the chopped onion and garlic until soft. Stir in the tomatoes and cook for another 10 minutes. Mash the tomatoes in the saucepan with a potato masher, then add the herbs, seasoning and flour. Stir in the sherry from the fish, add the bay leaf and breadcrumbs and cook for a couple of minutes more.

Pour the sauce over the fish and place in preheated, moderately hot oven for 25 minutes, until fish is cooked. Garnish with fresh parsley and serve immediately.

Serves 4.

"BIENMESABE" (CAZON EN ADOBO)

"It Tastes Good to Me"
Fried Marinated Tope or Baby Shark

As the name implies, this is a very tasty dish. It is a speciality of the Cadiz region of southern Spain where the semi-secret family recipes for the marinade are passed on from one generation to another. The fish is also sold already cooked in the *freidurías*, the Spanish equivalent of the British fish and chip shops. There is a great deal of rivalry among the *freidurías* as to which has the best marinade recipe for the *bienmesabe* and they guard their recipes jealously. The fish is usually coated in semolina before frying. However, if semolina is not available, all-purpose flour may be used. We are very happy to be able to share this recipe with you and hope it will become one of your favorites too—especially as it is very simple to make. As with the previous recipe, it is important that the shark used for this dish is the softer-textured baby shark.

As always, of course, the question of the marinade—the degree of sharpness and marinating time—is very much a matter of taste. After experimenting with several variations, our particular favorite is the following:

4 large (or 8 medium/small) baby shark steaks
semolina or all-purpose flour for coating
oil for frying

Marinade:

5 tablespoons white wine vinegar
12 tablespoons water
1 teaspoon ground cumin
½ teaspoon paprika
salt to taste
½ teaspoon oregano
2 bay leaves

Mix all the ingredients for the marinade and pour into large shallow dish. Place the fish in the marinade, cover with foil, place in the refrigerator and allow to stand for around 36 hours. Turn the fish occasionally.

Remove fish from the marinade and dry on a paper towel. Coat the fish in the semolina or all-purpose flour; when well-coated shake off excess. Then plunge the fish into deep hot oil in a frying pan. Cook for 4-5 minutes, or until golden in color.

Serves 4.

CHIORRO

Cod or Haddock, Basque-Style

This recipe for *chiorro* is just one of the many ways the succulent white fish of the Bay of Biscay is prepared and served in the Basque region.

4 steaks of white fish (cod, haddock or hake)
2 onions thinly sliced
2 cloves of garlic—finely chopped
2 teaspoons tomato paste/purée
1 cup red wine
1 cup water
1 teaspoon paprika
pinch of cayenne pepper
ground black pepper
1 tablespoon all-purpose flour
4 slices bread
4 teaspoons lemon juice
2 tablespoons water
½ cup olive oil
salt to taste

Put the fish into a well-greased ovenproof dish and season to taste. Combine the lemon juice and two tablespoons of water and pour over the fish. Then cover and cook in a moderate oven for about 20 minutes.

Meanwhile, make the sauce by frying the onions and garlic in 3-4 tablespoons of olive oil until soft. Add the flour, seasoning, paprika, cayenne pepper and tomato paste and stir well. Then add the wine and water, mix well and simmer for about 15 minutes.

Use the rest of the oil to fry the 4 slices of bread on both sides until golden brown and then place them on a serving dish.

Remove the fish from the oven and drain well. Place one

fish steak on each slice of bread and cover with the sauce. Serve immediately.

Serves 4.

LENGUADO ALFONSO XIII

Sole Alfonso XIII (with stuffed eggplant/aubergine)

This is an exquisite dish suitable for a special lunch or dinner party.

1½ lb skinned sole fillets
juice ½ lemon
2 eggplants/aubergines
½ cup sunflower oil (or other light oil)
3 tablespoons fresh breadcrumbs
1 tablespoon grated *manchego*, or other hard cheese
flour for coating
1 medium onion—peeled and chopped
2 medium-sized ripe tomatoes—peeled and chopped
1 clove garlic—chopped
1 teaspoon lemon thyme
1½ tablespoons butter
seasoning to taste

Stuffed Eggplants:

Cut eggplants in half lengthways. Then, without cutting through to the skin, make a few cuts with a knife in the eggplant flesh and sprinkle with salt. Leave for 30 minutes or so.

Sauté the onion until soft in 2 tablespoons of oil, then add the tomatoes, garlic, herbs and seasoning and continue cooking for a few more minutes.

Dry the eggplants. Heat about 3 tablespoons of oil in a large shallow pan and lay the eggplants (flesh-side down) in pan. Sauté until golden brown, adding a little more oil when necessary. Then, turn and fry on skin side for few minutes.

Lift eggplants out of pan and dry with a paper towel. Scoop out the flesh and chop. Mix this flesh with the onion and tomato mixture and cook for 2-3 minutes. Put the eggplant skins in greased, ovenproof dish and fill with the mixture. Combine the breadcrumbs and grated cheese and sprinkle on top. Put these into a preheated, moderately hot oven for a few minutes while you cook the sole.

Prepare the fish:

Dip the sole fillets in seasoned flour. Put the butter and one tablespoon of oil in a large shallow pan and heat, then fry the fish gently for a few minutes on each side until tender (add a little more oil when necessary). Remove and place one fillet on each of the eggplant halves. Sprinkle with lemon juice and serve immediately.

Serves 4.

LENGUADO AL JEREZ CON ESPECIES

Sole with Sherry and Spices

A delicious and delicately flavored dish which is both easy and quick to prepare.

4 large lemon sole fillets
5 tablespoons butter
2 tablespoons sunflower oil (or other light oil)
3 tablespoons *fino* dry sherry
1 teaspoon lemon juice
1 tablespoon orange juice
1 teaspoon mixed spices and herbs (for fish)
3 scallions/spring onions—chopped
1 tablespoon chopped parsley
seasoning to taste

Season the sole fillets with salt and pepper. Melt the butter in a large frying pan, add the oil, heat and sauté the fillets for 3-4 minutes on each side until lightly golden. Remove from pan, sprinkle with lemon juice and keep hot.

In the same pan, put the chopped scallions, spices and parsley and cook until the butter turns light brown. Stir in the sherry and orange juice and cook for an additional minute or so.

Spoon the spicy sauce over the fish and serve immediately.

Serve with creamed potatoes.

Serves 4.

LENGUADOS RELLENOS

Stuffed Fillet of Sole

This is another attractive sole dish which can be prepared in advance to the point where the fillets are wrapped in the foil. They then just need to be placed in the oven and cooked for about 25 minutes before serving.

4 large fillets of sole
½ cup mushrooms—chopped
½ cup cooked peeled shrimps/prawns (about 4 oz)
½ cup fresh breadcrumbs
½ cup finely chopped onion
¼ cup minced celery
1 egg—beaten
¼ cup white wine
3 tablespoons olive oil
seasoning to taste
1 lemon, cut into slices
fresh parsley to garnish

Put the oil into a large frying pan, add the onion and sauté until soft. Add the mushrooms, celery, breadcrumbs, shrimps and beaten egg, season to taste and mix well. Now divide the mixture into 4 parts; place one part in the center of each sole fillet and roll up. Secure with a fine skewer or cocktail stick.

Cut four pieces of aluminum foil (large enough to wrap the fillet) and brush each piece of foil with a little oil. Place the rolled fillet in the foil, pour 1 tablespoon of wine over each and place a slice of lemon on top. Fold the foil over the fillets and seal.

Place fish in a preheated, moderately hot oven and bake for about 25 minutes, until done. Then remove, place fish on serving dish and garnish with fresh parsley and lemon slices. Serve immediately.

Serves 4.

LOBINA EN SALSA COLORADA

Sea Bass in Red Sauce

This colorful dish is also good with hake, halibut or sea bass. We like to serve it with saffron rice and zucchini/courgettes.

4 large slices sea bass
1 tablespoon wine vinegar
2 cups water
seasoning to taste
bay leaf

Sauce:

1 tablespoon butter
1 tablespoon all-purpose flour
½ cup chopped mushrooms
1 teaspoon paprika
pinch cayenne pepper
1 tablespoon *fino* (dry) sherry
1 large canned sweet red pepper—cut into strips
1 cup milk
seasoning to taste

Put the water, vinegar, bay leaf and seasoning into a large, shallow pan; add the fish, cover and poach until tender (about 20 minutes)

Sauce:

Fry the mushrooms in the butter for a few minutes. Remove from heat and add the flour, paprika, cayenne pepper and milk. Mix well and return to heat, stirring constantly. Bring to boil and simmer for few minutes, then add the drained and sliced sweet red pepper and the sherry.

Remove fish from pan and drain well. Place on serving dish and spoon the sauce over.

Serves 4.

MEJILLONES CON LIMON AL VAPOR

Lemon Steamed Mussels

This recipe is one of the simplest ways of cooking mussels, and also happens to be our favorite.

3 lbs (approx.) fresh mussels
1 large lemon
2 tablespoons dry white wine (optional)
seasoning to taste

Cleaning mussels/clams:

When preparing fresh mussels, make sure that the shells are closed or, if slightly open, test to see if they are alive by tapping the shell with a knife; if the mussels are alive, the shells will close. Discard any open (dead) mussels.

The mussels should be scrubbed thoroughly. After scrubbing, wash the mussels in several waters—put them into a bowl of water and stir them with your hand; do not allow them to remain still. Then drain the mussels. Do this two or three times. Add a pinch of salt to the last water. The water should now be clear and free of sand.

Cut the lemon in half and squeeze out the juice. Put the lemon juice, the two halves of the squeezed lemon, the wine (if used), and plenty of seasoning into a large saucepan. Put the saucepan over a high heat and add the well-scrubbed mussels. Cook quickly over the strong heat, shaking the pan continuously, until all the mussels are open (around 3 minutes). Any mussels which do not open should be discarded.

Transfer the cooked mussels and juice to individual earthenware dishes and serve immediately.

Serves 4-6 as a starter.

MEJILLONES A LA MARINERA

Mussels with Wine, Garlic, Onion and Tomato Suace

This is probably the most popular way of cooking mussels. It makes a very tasty first course, served with lots of crusty bread.

3 lbs (approx.) fresh mussels
4 tablespoons chopped tomatoes
2 tablespoons fresh breadcrumbs
1 medium onion—chopped
2 cloves garlic—chopped
3 tablespoons oil
1 cup dry white wine
1 tablespoon chopped parsley
1 large lemon
seasoning to taste

Scrub the mussels thoroughly and wash in several waters, as indicated in the preceding recipe.

Put the oil into a large frying pan and sauté the onion and garlic until soft. Add the chopped tomatoes and breadcrumbs and stir until the mixture thickens to the consistency of thin cream. Set aside.

Put the wine and plenty of seasoning into a large saucepan and bring to the boil. Add the well-scrubbed mussels. Cover and cook for about 3-5 minutes, shaking the pan continuously, until all the mussels have opened. Using a perforated spoon, remove the mussels from the liquid and place them on a large dish. Discard the empty half of the shell and retain the half to which the mussels is attached. Discard any mussels which remain closed.

Strain the mussel liquid through a fine sieve or muslin, then add the strained liquid to the onion and tomato mixture. Bring to the boil, stirring continuously. Add a little salt and ground pepper to taste. Pour the hot sauce over the mussels, sprinkle with chopped parsley and serve immediately. Garnish with lemon slices.

Serves 4-6 as a starter.

Variation:

Clams may be substituted for mussels if preferred.

MERLUZA EN SALSA DE TOMATE Y ALMENDRAS

Hake in Tomato and Almond Sauce

This is a variation of a well-known hake dish served with a *marinera* sauce.

4 large hake fillets (about 7 oz each)
3 cups water
2 teaspoons lemon juice
3 peppercorns
2 slices of onion
salt to taste

For the Sauce:

1 medium onion—chopped

1 tablespoon parsley—finely chopped
1 clove garlic—finely chopped
pinch nutmeg
½ cup ground almonds
3 tablespoons fresh breadcrumbs
2 strips smoked bacon—diced
2 cups canned chopped tomatoes (1 medium can, 16 oz size)
3 tablespoons olive oil
seasoning to taste
few sprigs parsley to garnish

To Poach the Fish:

Put the water into a large, shallow pan and add the onion slices, peppercorns, salt and lemon juice. Cover, bring to the boil and simmer gently for about 10-15 minutes, until the fish is cooked.

When the fish is cooked, remove from the pan, drain, place on heated dish and keep hot. Do not discard the poaching liquid.

To Make the Sauce:

Put 3 tablespoons oil into a large, shallow pan, add the chopped onion and garlic and sauté until soft. Then, add the diced bacon and sauté for a couple of minutes. Incorporate the breadcrumbs and almonds and cook for an additional two minutes. Stir in the tomatoes, parsley and seasoning to taste, and add about 2 cups of the liquid in which the fish was poached. Turn up the heat, mix well and cook until the sauce begins to thicken and a creamy consistency is reached. Then spoon the sauce over the fish. Garnish with a few sprigs of parsley. Serve immediately with lots of crusty French bread to mop up the sauce.

Serves 4.

MERLUZA A LA VASCA
Hake, Basque-Style

Merluza a la vasca, which includes asparagus, peas and clams, is perhaps the best-known of the fish dishes from the Basque country. The rest of the ingredients are more or less the same as in many other hake dishes from this region and the addition of clams is optional, but, when available, most people like to include them.

4 large, firm hake steaks
1 small onion—finely chopped
1 clove of garlic—crushed
3 tablespoons olive oil
1½ tablespoons parsley—chopped
1 tablespoon all-purpose flour
1 cup water
½ cup dry white wine
8 small or 4 large fresh asparagus spears—cooked (or canned/frozen asparagus)
1 hard-boiled egg—chopped
1 cup peas—cooked
1 cup clams—well scrubbed and rinsed in several waters
seasoning to taste

Put the oil into a large, flameproof, (preferably) earthenware casserole or pan and sauté the garlic and onions until soft. Add the flour and 1 tablespoon of chopped parsley and mix well. Pour in the water, stir and allow to cook for a further 5 minutes. Add the hake steaks, seasoning to taste and the wine. Bring to the boil, then reduce heat immediately. Cover and simmer gently for about 15 minutes.

Then add the cooked asparagus spears, the peas and the clams to the casserole and allow to cook for around 5-8 minutes. Discard any clams which do not open. Before serving, garnish with the rest of the parsley and the chopped hard-boiled egg.

Serves 4.

MERO AL OLOROSO

Grouper in Oloroso Sherry

(If grouper is not available, monkfish, halibut or bass may be used.)

Mero, or grouper, is a succulent fish, which is very highly regarded in Spain. In fact, there is a Spanish saying which honors it as being the best in the sea: *Del mar el mero, de la tierra el carnero* (From the sea grouper [is the best]; from the land, ram).

Oloroso is a rich, dark (but not too sweet) sherry. A good *oloroso* has a velvety consistency combined with a tangy, nutty flavor. This means that as well as being a delicious drink, it also lends a different and rather special flavor to your cooking. We have also made this dish very successfully with sea bass and bream, but a good-sized grouper cannot be beaten. However, they are all very tasty and the dish could not be simpler to make.

4 large fillets/slices of grouper
3 tablespoons *oloroso* sherry
1 generous cup water
2 tablespoons heavy/double cream
rind of one lemon
2 teaspoons butter
2 teaspoons all-purpose flour
seasoning to taste
bay leaf

Place the fish in a large, shallow pan with the sherry, lemon rind, seasoning, water and bay leaf. Cover and poach for about 15 minutes until tender. Then remove the fish from the liquid and discard any skin. Melt the butter in a pan and stir in the flour to form a paste. Then, stirring constantly, slowly add the strained poaching stock and simmer gently for a couple of minutes. Lower heat and stir in the cream. Put the fish back into the pan and gently heat through in the sauce, but do not allow the sauce to boil. The sauce should have the consistency of light cream.

Serve immediately.

We like to serve it with rice and peas or flat beans.

Serves 4.

PEZ ESPADA CON ESPARRAGOS Y PATATAS

Swordfish with Asparagus and Potatoes

Swordfish is very popular throughout Spain, and this dish makes quite a substantial main course.

4 large slices swordfish
1 onion—chopped
8-10 fresh asparagus spears
6 medium potatoes
1 cup mushrooms
3 medium-sized ripe tomatoes—peeled and chopped
pinch each of paprika and cumin
¼ cup red wine
¼ cup water
seasoning to taste
2 teaspoons fresh basil—chopped
bay leaf
6 tablespoons olive oil
¼ teaspoon all-purpose flour

First prepare the asparagus and potatoes. Peel the potatoes and boil in salted water for 5 minutes. Wash asparagus, cut off the tough end parts and cook in boiling, salted water for five minutes. Remove potatoes and asparagus and drain. Cut the asparagus in half. Cut the potatoes into medium-thick slices.

Sauté the fish in about 4 tablespoons of oil for a couple of minutes on each side. Remove from pan. Then add the chopped onions, asparagus, seasoning and herbs to the pan and sauté until onions are soft.

Cover the bottom of a greased, ovenproof dish with the potato slices (use all the potatoes). Place the fish on top. Then cover the fish with the onion and asparagus mixture.

Fry the mushrooms in the remaining oil, add one teaspoon flour and mix well. Stir in the tomatoes, wine, water, paprika and cumin, and pour over the fish in the casserole. Place the casserole in a preheated, moderately hot oven for 35-40 minutes.

Serves 4.

PEZ ESPADA CON PEPINO Y CREMA DE AZAFRAN

Swordfish with Cucumber and Saffron Cream Sauce

The saffron cream sauce and cucumber marry very well with the rich, meaty fish. We like to serve this dish with mint potatoes and flat beans.

4 good-sized slices swordfish
pinch ground saffron
pinch of yellow food coloring
2 lemons
½ cup of thick/whipping cream
1 large cucumber
1½ tablespoons butter
1 tablespoon chopped fresh parsley
seasoning to taste

Grate the rind and squeeze the juice of one lemon. Place the fish in a flameproof casserole or large frying pan, add the lemon juice, rind, seasoning and enough water to cover the fish. Poach gently until tender (about 10-15 minutes). Then remove the fish and drain. Cover the fish and place in a heated oven to keep warm.

Cut the cucumber into thick, chunky pieces and sauté in the melted butter until just soft.

Meanwhile, whip the cream and add the saffron, coloring, parsley, a few drops of lemon juice and a pinch of salt and mix well.

Remove the fish from the oven and place on a serving dish. Arrange the cucumber around the dish and put a spoonful of the thick cream sauce in the center of each steak and gently spread lengthways with a fork. Garnish with lemon slices and fresh parsley. Serve immediately.

Serves 4.

PEZ ESPADA CON CAPA ALEGRE

Swordfish with "Happy" Topping

This dish is so called because of the bright colorful topping which accompanies it. It makes a delicious main course at any time of the year. We like to serve it with saffron rice.

4 large slices of swordfish
juice and grated rind of ½ large lemon
1 generous cup water
2 large ripe tomatoes—chopped
1 medium onion
2 medium zucchini/courgettes
1 large sweet red pepper
3-4 tablespoons sunflower oil (or other light oil)
1 tablespoon parsley—chopped
seasoning to taste

Put the swordfish in an ovenproof dish and add the water mixed with lemon juice, rind and seasoning. Cover with foil and cook in preheated, moderate oven for approximately 25 minutes, until the fish is tender and breaks apart.

While the fish is cooking, prepare the *capa* or topping:

Chop the onion, red pepper and zucchini, season and sauté in the oil until soft. Add the chopped tomatoes and cook for an additional 4-5 minutes.

Remove the fish from the oven, drain and place on serving dish. Spoon the colorful sauce over the fish slices and sprinkle with fresh parsley.

Serves 4.

PUDIN DE PESCADO
Fish Pie

The word *pudin* is an adaptation of the English word *pudding*. In English this usually refers to a sweet dish, but in Spanish it refers to dishes using a variety of ingredients—either savory or sweet, but mainly savory—which are then combined to make a type of pie. This *pudin de pescado* is one simple, but delicious, example of many other savory *pudines*. It is also a very versatile dish as it can be served hot with white sauce, or a rich tomato sauce, or cold with hardboiled eggs and mayonnaise. It can be served as a starter or as a main course.

1 lb firm white fish (cod, hake, haddock)
1 cup water
2 teaspoons lemon juice
2 slices bread—crusts removed
¾ cup milk
2 large eggs
3 tablespoons *fino* (dry) sherry or white wine

2 teaspoons butter
seasoning to taste
pinch nutmeg

Put the fish into a large, shallow pan with the water, lemon juice and a pinch of salt and poach for about 10 minutes. Remove fish from the pan and drain, discarding any bones or skin. Flake the fish very finely. Soak the bread in the milk, and when the milk has been absorbed, squeeze out excess liquid. Then add the bread to the fish. Mix in the sherry or wine (we prefer sherry), butter, nutmeg and seasoning. When all this is very well mixed, add the well-beaten egg yolks. Then beat egg whites until stiff and fold into mixture. Put this into greased ovenproof dish. Place in preheated, moderately hot oven for 15-20 minutes.

This can be served cold or hot as mentioned above.

Serves 3-4.

Variation:

Leave out the nutmeg and, before adding the egg yolks, mix in 1 tablespoon tomato paste/purée, then proceed as above.

PUDIN DE MERLUZA

Hake Pudding

This dish is simple and quick to prepare. Cod or haddock may be substituted for hake and it makes an ideal first course. We like to serve it with fresh beets, *zanahorias aliñadas* (carrots in vinagrette) and fresh, crusty bread.

¾ lb hake fillets
2 tablespoons *fino* (dry) sherry
2 medium slices bread—crusts removed
seasoning to taste
3 tablespoons olive oil

2 crushed garlic cloves
1 tablespoon lemon juice
1 cup water
¼ cup milk
few stuffed olives for garnish

Place the fish in a shallow pan with the water, seasoning and 1 tablespoon lemon juice and poach for about 15 minutes until cooked. Gently remove the fish and put on a plate, discard any skin or bones.

Soak the bread in the milk until soft.

Flake fish as finely as possible with a fork. Squeeze excess liquid from the bread and mash the bread with the back of a spoon. Add the bread to the flaked fish and beat with a fork until a soft and smooth consistency. Slowly, mix in the garlic, olive oil and seasoning, then beat in the sherry. Place in a serving dish and put in the refrigerator to chill for two hours. Garnish with a few stuffed olives.

Serves 4 as a starter.

RAPE EN SALSA DE ALMENDRAS

Monkfish in Almond Sauce

This is a famous and classic Spanish dish. It is ideal for a dinner party and can be prepared in advance and simply placed in the oven about 15 minutes before serving.

4 large slices of monkfish (about 7-8 oz each)
1 medium onion
¼ cup fresh breadcrumbs
2 cloves of garlic—chopped
1 tablespoon chopped parsley
½ cup of ground almonds
½ cup water or fish stock
½ (generous) cup white wine

1 cup canned chopped tomatoes (about 8oz)
½ cup sunflower oil, or other light oil
pinch of ground saffron
seasoning to taste

Gently sauté the fish in about 4 tablespoons of oil for a couple of minutes on both sides, then transfer the fish to a greased, ovenproof dish.

Sauté the garlic, parsley, breadcrumbs and almonds in the same oil for 2-3 minutes (add a little more oil if necessary). Remove pan from heat, add the saffron and mix well. Then mash this mixture to a paste.

Put 2 tablespoons of oil into a shallow pan and sauté the chopped onions until soft, add the tomatoes and cook for an additional 5 minutes. Incorporate the crushed garlic/almond/parsley/bread mixture and stir in the wine and water. Season to taste. Bring to simmering point and then pour this sauce over the monkfish in the dish. Cover, and place this in a moderately hot oven for about 20 minutes, until the fish is cooked.

Garnish with fresh parsley and lemon slices and serve with lots of crusty bread.

Serves 4.

RAPE CON SALSA FUERTE

Monkfish with Tangy Sauce

This firm-textured fish combines very well with the crunchy nuts, and the slightly tangy sauce makes this dish something special. The recipe is equally good with hake, bream or sea bass.

4 large slices of monkfish
¼ cup orange juice
grated rind of one large orange

1 clove garlic
2 large ripe tomatoes—peeled and chopped
3 tablespoons olive oil
¼ cup chopped walnuts
½ cup dry white wine
seasoning to taste
few drops lemon juice

Garnish:
1 lemon cut into wedges
1 orange—sliced

Put the oil into a large, shallow frying pan or casserole and sauté the chopped onions and garlic until soft. Add the chopped tomatoes, wine, walnuts, orange juice, rind and seasoning. Cook for additional three minutes. Then add the monkfish portions, cover and cook over medium heat until tender (approx. 15 minutes). When cooked, place the fish on serving dish, spoon the sauce over, sprinkle with fresh parsley and a few drops of lemon juice. Garnish with orange slices and lemon wedges.

Serves 4.

RAYA VALENCIANA

Skate Valencian Style

Though a strange looking fish, skate has a surprisingly delicate flavor, and this recipe from Valencia, with its slightly piquant sauce, makes a pleasant change from the usual fried or grilled skate dishes.

2 lbs skate
2-3 cups water
pinch salt
1½ tablespoons white wine vinegar
1 bay leaf

pinch each of cumin and paprika
3 peppercorns
½ onion—sliced

Sauce:
1 tablespoon butter
1 medium onion—chopped
2 teaspoons honey
¾ cup orange juice
1 teaspoon chopped parsley
1 tablespoon brandy (optional)
1½ teaspoons lemon juice

To cook skate:

Put the water, salt to taste, white wine vinegar, bay leaf, cumin and paprika, peppercorns and half a sliced onion in a pan and bring to boil. Add the skate and simmer gently for 25 minutes.

Meanwhile, make the sauce:

Melt the butter in a pan and fry the chopped onion until soft. Add the orange juice and honey and cook for a couple of minutes. Then add the lemon juice, parsley and seasoning. Bring to boil, stir in the brandy and cook for couple of minutes.

Remove the fish carefully from pan and drain. Discard any skin. Put the fish on serving dish, pour the sauce over and serve immediately.

Serves 4.

RODABALLO CON VINO BLANCO AL HORNO

Baked Brill in White Wine

Brill is another fine-textured, delectable white fish, and this full-flavored dish makes an admirable main course. We like to serve it with fried, sliced eggplant/aubergine.

4 large brill fillets—trimmed and skinned
2 medium onions—chopped
4 medium-sized ripe tomatoes—peeled and chopped
1 clove garlic—chopped
1 large green pepper—chopped
1 cup mushrooms—chopped
¾ cup dry white wine
5-6 tablespoons olive oil
2 teaspoons fresh parsley—chopped
2 tablespoons fresh breadcrumbs
½ teaspoon dried mixed herbs
2 teaspoons all-purpose flour
seasoning to taste
few drops lemon juice

Put 3 tablespoons of oil into a large, shallow pan and sauté the onions, green pepper and garlic in the oil until soft, then add the flour and mix well. Transfer these vegetables to an ovenproof dish (large enough to hold all the vegetables and the fish fillets). Place the fish slices on top of the onion and green pepper mixture.

Now sauté the mushrooms in the remaining oil for a couple of minutes, add the chopped tomatoes, parsley, herbs, breadcrumbs and seasoning to the mushrooms and mix well. Spoon this mixture over the fish. Pour in the wine around the edge of the dish and sprinkle the top with a few drops lemon juice.

Cover with foil and place in preheated, moderately hot oven. Cook for about 25-30 minutes until the fish is tender.

Serves 4.

RODABALLO CON CALABACINES

Brill with Zucchini/Courgettes

This is a very agreeable and unfussy dish in which the

brill fillets are poached gently in a court bouillon and served in a simple sauce made from the poaching liquid. We often substitute lightly sautéed diced cucumber for the zucchini.

4 large brill fillets
juice and rind of ½ lemon
¾ cup water
3 peppercorns
1 tablespoon butter
1 tablespoon all-purpose flour
4 zucchini/courgettes
1 teaspoon dill—chopped
1 cup milk
3-4 tablespoons olive oil
seasoning to taste

Place the fish in a large, shallow pan with the water, juice and rind of half a lemon, peppercorns and pinch salt. Bring to simmering point, cover and poach for 15 minutes. Then remove the fish carefully and keep hot.

Wash and dry zucchini, cut into medium-thick slices, season, add dill and sauté in the oil until tender (about 8 minutes).

Meanwhile, melt the butter in a pan and stir in the flour, mix to a paste and slowly add the poaching liquid from the fish, together with the milk. Cook rapidly, stirring continuously, to reduce liquid to creamy consistency.

Place the fish on a serving dish, spoon the sauce over. Garnish with the sautéed zucchini and the lemon slices.

Serves 4.

SALTEADO RAPIDO DE CHAMPIÑONES Y GAMBAS

Mushrooms and Shrimps/Prawns "Rápido"

This uncomplicated, tasty dish makes an ideal first course. It is also suitable for the main course of a light lunch or supper.

2 cups roughly chopped mushrooms (about ½ lb)
1½ cups cooked, peeled shrimp/prawns
3 ripe tomatoes—chopped
3 slices smoked bacon—chopped
1 zucchini/courgette
1 teaspoon chopped fresh tarragon
1 tablespoon *amontillado* sherry
juice of ½ orange
3-4 tablespoons oil
seasoning to taste

Wash zucchini and mushrooms, then dry on a paper towel and cut into chunky pieces. Put the oil into a large shallow pan and sauté the mushrooms and zucchini pieces for about five minutes. Add the bacon, tomatoes, tarragon and seasoning and continue cooking for a few more minutes. Stir in the shrimp and add the orange juice and sherry. Cook an additional two to three minutes.

Serve on a bed of rice.

Serves 4 as a starter, or 2 as a main course.

TRUCHA A LA NAVARRA

Navarre-Style Trout

This is a classic dish from the old kingdom of Navarre, in the north of Spain. Situated at the foot of the Pyrenees, the rivers and streams of its beautiful valleys are renowned for their freshwater fish—particularly trout. The freshness and delicacy of the fish from this region means that it requires only the simplest form of cooking.

4 fresh trout
seasoning to taste
4 tablespoons sunflower oil, or other light oil
4 thin slices of *serrano*, or other cured ham
all-purpose flour for dredging
parsley to garnish
1 lemon—cut into wedges

Wash and clean the trout and dry on a paper towel, sprinkle with salt and allow to stand for 15-20 minutes.

Insert a slice of ham inside each trout. Then close, secure with a wooden cocktail stick and dredge with flour.

Heat the oil in a large frying pan and sauté the trout for a few minutes on each side until cooked and golden in color. Garnish with lemon wedges and parsley and serve immediately.

Serves 4.

TRUCHAS CON JAMON Y ALMENDRAS
Trout with Cured Ham and Almonds

This is a variation of *Trucha a la Navarra*

4 fresh trout
4 thin slices *serrano*, or other cured ham
1 tablespoon diced cured ham
1 tablespoon chopped parsley
1 tablespoon *fino* dry sherry
2 tablespoons chopped almonds
1 teaspoon lemon juice
5 tablespoons oil for frying
all-purpose flour for dredging
seasoning to taste

Sprinkle the cleaned and dried trout with salt and allow to stand for 15-20 minutes. Insert a slice of ham inside each trout. Then close, secure with a wooden cocktail pick and dredge with flour.

Heat 3-4 tablespoons of oil in a large frying pan and sauté the trout for a few minutes on each side until cooked, then transfer the fish to an ovenproof dish.

In another pan sauté the almonds, parsley and chopped ham in the remaining oil until lightly golden in color. Stir in the sherry, seasoning and lemon juice and mix well, then pour this over the trout. Place the fish in a moderately hot oven for about 8-10 minutes. Serve immediately.

Serves 4.

URTA AL COÑAC
Porgy in Brandy

Urta is a delectable fish with firm white flesh and an excellent flavor. It is a type of *pargo* (red snapper or porgy) found in the Atlantic waters near Cádiz. *Urta al coñac* is a dish we choose whenever we see it on a local menu.

4 medium pieces of porgy
2 tablespoons brandy
2 tablespoons butter
2 tablespoons white wine
6 tablespoons canned chopped tomatoes
2 teaspoons tomato paste/purée
parsley to garnish
1 lemon—cut into wedges
seasoning to taste

Put the butter into a large, shallow pan and sauté the lightly seasoned porgy for a couple of minutes on each side. Pour the brandy over and set alight. When the flame subsides, transfer the fish to a greased ovenproof dish. Mix together the chopped tomatoes, tomato paste and white wine, then pour this over the fish. Season to taste, cover with foil and place in preheated, moderate oven for 20-25 minutes, until cooked and browned.

Garnish with fresh parsley and lemon wedges.

Serve with sautéed potatoes.

Serves 4.

ZARZUELA DE PESCADO O DE MARISCOS

OPERETTA OF FISH STEW OR SHELLFISH

Zarzuela is the name of a type of operetta which is uniquely Spanish—as its themes, both dramatic and musical, are rooted in the country's folklore. It takes its name from the Zarzuela Palace, the residence of the Spanish Monarch, where these musical works were first performed. The palace itself was so called because, when it was first built on the outskirts of Madrid in the seventeenth century, the area was covered with brambles, or *zarzas*, and *zarzuela* is a diminutive of *zarza*—hence the name: *El Palacio de la Zarzuela* or The Little Bramble Palace.

Zarzuela de pescado (fish stew operetta) and *zarzuela de mariscos* (operetta of seafood) do not contain any brambles whatsoever. But the imaginative use of the name in these dishes immediately brings to mind the colorful folklore, lively harmonies and variety of textures that are the hallmarks of the Spanish operetta.

ZARZUELA DE PESCADO

Fish Stew Operetta

The dish is very versatile lending itself to improvisation and many variations according to taste and budget. This recipe for *zarzuela de pescado* is our version and it is one of our favorite main course dishes for a dinner party.

We like to serve it in large individual earthenware dishes which keep the food hot and in which the shellfish and juices are more easily manageable.

2 swordfish steaks
2 hake steaks (or cod or haddock)
½ lb squid—cleaned and cut into pieces
1 cup peeled, cooked shrimp/prawns
8-10 uncooked large prawn tails or king prawns
2 large onions—chopped
2 green peppers—chopped
2 cloves garlic—chopped
4 tablespoons canned chopped tomatoes
1 cup peas (fresh or frozen)
2 cups fish stock
1 teaspoon anchovy paste/purée
2 tablespoons brandy
seasoning to taste
1 teaspoon dried mixed herbs
½ cup oil

Pour half the oil into a frying pan and sauté the onions, peppers and garlic until tender. Stir in the mixed herbs and tomatoes.

Cut the fish steaks in half.

In another large pan (with lid) put the remaining oil and gently sauté the squid, hake and swordfish slices for a few minutes on each side. Pour the brandy into a very small pan and heat gently, then light and pour the flaming brandy over the fish. When the flame has subsided, add the onion and tomato mixture to the fish in the large pan and stir well. Pour in the fish stock, incorporate the anchovy paste, season to taste, cover and cook over low heat for 15 minutes. Then add the uncooked prawn tails (with shells) and peas and cook for additional 5-10 minutes. Two minutes before serving, add the cooked peeled shrimps and heat through.

Serve the stew in individual earthenware dishes with lots of crusty bread.

Serves 4.

ZARZUELA DE MARISCOS

Operetta of Seafood

Another delicious seafood dish. The basic difference between this and the *zarzuela de pescado* above is that this dish has more shellfish and less white fish. It also includes ground almonds.

1 lb small peeled raw shrimp/prawns
12-18 raw king prawns with shells (or half quantity of king prawns, plus 2 rock lobster tails cut into thirds)
1 lb firm white fish—cut into medium-thick slices
12-18 mussels—well scrubbed
2 cloves garlic—chopped
1 medium onion—chopped
6 tablespoons olive oil
1 red pepper—seeded and chopped
3 medium tomatoes—peeled and chopped
¼ cup ground blanched almonds
2 cups fish stock
½ cup white wine
2 tablespoons brandy
seasoning to taste
1 tablespoon chopped parsley
good pinch ground saffron
lemon wedges to garnish

Wash and scrub the mussels as indicated on p. 127.

Pour half the oil into a frying pan and sauté the onions, peppers and garlic until soft and set aside.

Put the remaining oil into another large pan or flameproof casserole and gently sauté the fish slices for 2-3 minutes on each side until lightly golden. Heat the brandy in a very small pan and set alight, then pour the flaming brandy over the fish. When the flame has subsided, add the onion, pepper and garlic mixture to the fish, then incorporate the almonds, tomatoes, saffron, parsley and seasoning and mix well. Pour in the wine and stock, bring to the boil and add the peeled shrimps and the large prawns in their shells and lobster tails (if used). Reduce heat and simmer for about 5 minutes. Add the scrubbed mussels and allow to simmer for an additional 10 minutes, until the mussels have opened and the sauce has reduced slightly. Discard any unopened mussels, garnish with lemon wedges and serve immediately with plenty of crusty French bread.

Serves 4 to 6.

ARENQUES EN ESCABECHE

Soused Herrings

In this dish from Huelva, southwest Spain, the prepared herrings are left for 2 days in a fairly mild wine vinegar marinade, the result is therefore not so acidy or harsh as many other dishes using stronger marinades.

6-8 fresh herrings (cleaned and filleted)
2 onions
1 carrot
½ cup pitted green olives
1 small horseradish root
¼ cup sugar
2 teaspoons pickling spice
generous pinch salt

¾ cup good quality white wine vinegar
3 bay leaves
¼ cup water

Slice the peeled onions and carrot very thinly. Place water and vinegar in a saucepan and bring to boil. Add the onions, carrots and salt and cook for 5 minutes, then add the sugar and heat until the sugar has dissolved completely. Allow liquid to cool.

Peel and grate the horseradish. Immerse the herrings in boiling water for a minute or two then remove and scrape away skins. Place the herrings, pickling spice, horseradish, bay leaves and sliced olives in a large shallow dish. Pour the vinegar and vegetables over. Cover and chill for at least 48 hours. Turn the herrings occasionally.

Serves 6.

ESCABECHE DE PESCADO

Pickled Fish

Another delicious spiced, pickled dish which uses firm-textured white fish.

1½ lb firm white fish slices (e.g., halibut, cod, sea bass, grouper)
2 onions—peeled and thinly sliced
2 carrots—scraped and grated
2 cloves of garlic—chopped
3 bay leaves
¾ cup good quality white wine vinegar
½ cup water
good pinch salt
small pinch each of ground black pepper, saffron, cumin, cinnamon, dried hot red pepper
2 cloves

scant ½ cup olive oil

The marinade:

Sauté the onions in 3 tablespoons of olive oil until soft, then add carrots, spices, bay leaves, garlic, vinegar, water and salt. Cook for five minutes.

To cook the fish:

Sauté the fish slices in about 4 tablespoons of oil for few minutes on each side, until tender. Remove the fish and drain on paper towel. Discard any bones or skin.

Place the fish in large shallow dish and pour the vinegar marinade over. Cover and chill for 48 hours.

Serves 6 as starter.

CARNES

Meats

CALLOS A LA MADRILEÑA
Tripe, Madrid-Style

As well as being a substantial main course, *callos a la madrileña* is also a very popular tapa dish, particularly in the Madrid area. It is one of the few Spanish recipes that specifies the use of a small amount of dried hot chili. Many people prefer to make this dish a day in advance and reheat it before serving.

2½ lbs tripe
1 pig's trotter
2 cloves garlic—chopped
medium onions—chopped
2 small *chorizos*, or substitute garlic sausage (about 4 oz)
2 *morcillas*, or substitute blood sausage (about 4 oz)
1 tablespoon oil
1 cup dry white wine
1 bay leaf

pinch of nutmeg
2 teaspoons paprika
2 cloves
1 small dried hot chili pepper—chopped
3 medium-sized ripe tomatoes—peeled and chopped
water
ground black pepper
seasoning to taste

Cut the tripe into large pieces and put into a saucepan with the pig's trotter, salt to taste and enough water to cover. Bring to the boil, cover and simmer for about 1 hour.

Then drain and cut the tripe into strips. Put the tripe strips, the trotter and the wine into a large, heavy pan (or pressure cooker), add enough water to cover and bring to the boil.

Add the bay leaf, whole *morcillas*, chopped chili, nutmeg, onion, garlic, tomatoes, black pepper, the cloves and salt to taste. Cover and allow to simmer gently for about 2 hours (if using a pressure cooker, reduce time accordingly).

Cut the *chorizos* into slices. Heat the oil in the frying pan, add the *chorizo* slices and the paprika and sauté gently for a couple of minutes. Add this to the tripe in the large pan and allow to cook for an additional hour or so.

Before serving, remove the meat from the pig's trotter, discard the bones and cut the meat into small pieces. Cut the *morcillas* into slices. Then return the meat and sausage to the pan and stir well.

Serves 6 as a main course.

CERDO / PORK

CINTA DE CERDO CON ACELGAS Y PIMIENTOS
Pork Fillet with Celery and Red Peppers

This dish is quick and easy to make. We prefer to use

green coriander, instead of parsley, as it seems to combine particularly well with the sweet red peppers.

2 lbs pork fillet/tenderloin—cut into cubes
2 sweet red peppers—deseeded and cut into strips
5 stalks celery—cut into medium-sized pieces
3 tablespoons sunflower oil, or other light oil
1 tablespoon lard or butter
1 teaspoon each paprika and cumin
1 tablespoon green coriander—chopped
1 cup chicken stock
¾ cup white wine
1 heaped teaspoon cornstarch/corn flour
seasoning to taste

Heat the oil and lard/butter in a large, heavy frying pan or casserole and quickly brown the pork. Reduce heat, add the peppers and celery, mix well and allow to cook for an additional 2 minutes. Add the herbs and spices, stock, wine and seasoning. Cover and allow to simmer gently for 10 minutes. Then, mix the cornstarch with a little cold water and add this to the pan, stirring constantly until the sauce thickens. Cover and continue cooking gently for an additional 10 minutes.

Serves 4.

COSTILLAS A LA EXTREMEÑA

Glazed Spare Ribs, Extremaduran-Style

We were served this dish for the first time in a small family-run restaurant in Cáceres in the region of Extremadura. The sweetness of the unusually large quantity of honey used is offset by the mustard, vinegar and fruit juices.

3½ lbs pork spare ribs—cut into separate ribs

½ teaspoon ground ginger
2 teaspoons paprika
1 large sweet red pepper—deseeded and cut into strips
1 onion—cut into pieces
3 tablespoons wine vinegar
2 teaspoons prepared mild mustard
4 tablespoons clear honey
2 tablespoons *oloroso,* medium sweet sherry
juice of 2 oranges
1 tablespoon lemon juice
salt to taste

Put the ribs in a roasting pan and sprinkle with salt. Place in preheated, moderately hot oven for about 30 minutes. (You may need to pour off some of the fat from the pork from time to time.)

Meanwhile, put the honey, mustard, 1 tablespoon of orange juice, the lemon juice, 1 tablespoon of sherry, paprika and the ginger into a saucepan, stir gently and melt the honey over a moderate heat. Pour half the thick honey sauce mixture over the ribs in the oven and continue cooking at a slightly lower temperature for an additional 30 minutes.

In the meantime, stir the rest of the orange juice, sherry and the vinegar into the remaining honey mixture. Add the onion and pepper pieces; cover and simmer gently for about 15 minutes.

When the ribs are cooked, place them on a serving dish and pour over the sauce. Serve immediately.

Serves 4-6.

COCHINILLO ASADO

Roast Suckling Pig

A good suckling pig should be about 6 weeks old. It will

need to be cooked for approximately 30 minutes per pound and basted often during cooking. Brushing with olive oil before cooking helps to give a crisper crackling.

In some of the best restaurants in Spain, particularly in Old Castile, the cooked suckling pig is cut with the edge of a plate, instead of a knife, as a demonstration of the meat's tenderness.

One 6 lb (approx.) suckling pig
¼ cup olive oil
salt
1 cup dry white wine
1½ tablespoons fresh mixed herbs

Clean the pig thoroughly before cooking and dry with paper towels. Cut the pig in half lengthways. Sprinkle the carcass with salt and set aside for 2 hours.

Sprinkle the inside with herbs such as thyme, parsley and tarragon. Brush the carcass generously with olive oil and place the pig in a large roasting pan. Put into a preheated, moderate oven and baste every 15 minutes with the fat and juices. After about 1½ hours pour the wine over the carcass and continue cooking for an additional 1½ hours, still basting every 15-20 minutes.

Cut the pig into slices and serve immediately.

Serves 4-6.

COCHINILLO ASADO CON SALSA DE JEREZ Y PASAS

Roast Suckling Pig with Sherry and Sultana Sauce

In Spain, suckling pig is usually eaten without any accompanying sauce other than its own juices. However, we sometimes like to serve it with a simple sherry and sultana/golden raisin sauce.

One 6 lb (approx.) suckling pig
¼ cup olive oil
salt
1 cup dry white wine
1½ tablespoons fresh mixed herbs

Sherry and Sultana Sauce:
2 tablespoons *amontillado,* medium dry sherry
1 tablespoon water
¼ cup sultanas/golden raisins
2 teaspoons sugar
juices from meat

Cook the pig as indicated in the previous recipe for *cochinillo asado.*

While the pig is cooking, make the sauce by soaking the sultanas in the sherry for about 1 hour. Then transfer them to a saucepan with the sugar and water and heat gently to melt the sugar. Add the juices from the cooked pig in the roasting pan. Mix well and allow to cook for a couple of minutes.

Cut the pig into slices and serve immediately with the hot sauce.

Serves 4 to 6.

CHULETAS DE CERDO A LA RIOJANA
Rioja-Style Pork Chops

This is a delicious, succulent dish which is quick and easy to prepare. Some people prefer to use flat-leaf parsley instead of coriander.

4 large pork loin chops
4 tablespoons oil
1 clove garlic—chopped

1 onion—chopped
3 sweet red peppers—seeded and chopped
2 medium-sized ripe tomatoes—peeled and chopped
4 tablespoons red wine
1 tablespoon green coriander—chopped
seasoning to taste

Heat the oil in a large, heavy frying pan and brown the chops quickly on both sides. Add the chopped garlic, onions and peppers and cook over a moderate heat until soft. Stir in the tomatoes, wine and coriander and add seasoning to taste. Cover and allow to simmer gently for about 20-25 minutes.

Serves 4.

CHULETAS DE CERDO CON ESPINACAS

Braised Pork Chops with Puréed Spinach

This is a very tasty way of cooking pork. The puréed spinach turns what could be a very ordinary dish into something special.

4 large pork loin chops
3 tablespoons oil
1 clove garlic—chopped
1 small onion—chopped
1 tablespoon chopped parsley
pinch nutmeg
¼ cup red wine
1 teaspoon prepared mild mustard
1 lb spinach—coarsely chopped
seasoning to taste
flour for dredging
migas or croutons

Dredge the chops with seasoned flour. Heat the oil in a large, shallow pan and quickly brown the chops. Transfer the chops to an ovenproof casserole dish.

Then add the chopped onion, garlic and parsley to the oil in the pan and sauté until soft. Stir in the mustard, nutmeg, spinach, seasoning to taste and the wine. Cover and simmer for about 5 minutes.

Put the ingredients in an electric blender and process to a smooth green purée. Spoon the purée over the chops in the casserole. Cover and place in a preheated, moderately hot oven for about 20-25 minutes.

Serve topped with *migas* or croutons.

Serves 4.

FILETES DE CERDO A LA ASTURIANA
Asturian-Style Pork Fillets

This dish from Spain's apple and cider region is a great favorite of ours. The tartness of the apple combines with the saltiness of the cured ham to give a subtly distinctive flavor.

8 thin slices pork fillet
1 medium onion—finely chopped
½ cooking apple—peeled, cored and chopped
2 tablespoons fresh breadcrumbs
1½ teaspoons sugar
pinch nutmeg
1 cup cider
¾ cup chicken stock
1 tablespoon fresh tarragon—chopped
3 tablespoons (approx. 1½ oz) cured ham—chopped
1 tablespoon all-purpose flour
rind of 1 lemon—grated
1 beaten egg
¼ cup oil
seasoning to taste

Heat 2 tablespoons oil in a large, shallow pan and fry the onion until soft. Add the apple, sugar, nutmeg, cured ham, lemon rind and tarragon and continue cooking over a moderate heat for 2 minutes. Stir in 1 tablespoon of cider and cook for an additional 2-3 minutes. Add the breadcrumbs, seasoning and the beaten egg and mix well. Divide the stuffing into 8 portions.

Beat the pork fillets with a mallet or heavy knife, if necessary. Then put one portion of the stuffing on each scallop, roll and secure with a cocktail stick.

Put the remaining oil into a frying pan and brown the meat lightly all over. Remove the pork and keep hot.

Add the flour to the oil in the pan and mix. Then stir in the rest of the cider and the stock and seasoning to taste. Put the pork back into the pan, cover and simmer gently for about 35 minutes, until the pork is tender.

Serves 4.

LOMO DE CERDO CON CIRUELAS PASAS

Pork with Prunes

This is another simple, but succulent way of cooking pork. It is usually served with sautéed or creamed potatoes. The prunes and sauce transform what could be a run-of-the-mill dish into a delicate and honeyed delight.

½ lb prunes
4 large (8 small) slices of pork fillet (about 1½ lb)
1 cup red wine
2 level teaspoons cornstarch/corn flour
1 cinnamon stick
2 teaspoons sugar
1 tablespoon lard or butter
2 tablespoons oil

1 tablespoon parsley—chopped
flour for dredging
water
warm tea (optional)
seasoning to taste

Put the prunes into a bowl, cover with water (or warm tea) and soak overnight.

Drain and put the prunes into a saucepan with the wine, cinnamon stick, sugar and enough water to just cover and simmer for 30 minutes.

Meanwhile, coat the pork in seasoned flour. Heat the lard/butter and oil in a large, shallow pan and sauté the pork gently until tender (about 5-8 minutes each side). Remove and keep hot.

When the prunes are cooked, lift out of the liquid with a perforated spoon and keep hot.

Make the sauce:

Drain some of the fat from the pan in which the pork was cooked and then add the strained liquid from the prunes. Mix the cornstarch with a little cold water and stir into the sauce. Season to taste. Cook over moderate heat, stirring constantly, until the sauce thickens.

Place the pork on a heated serving dish, arrange the prunes around and pour over the sauce. Serve immediately.

Serves 4.

LOMO AHUMADO EN SALSA DE CIRUELAS

Cured Pork Loin Steaks with Plum Sauce

We like to serve this simple but original dish with fried eggplant/aubergine and a mixed salad.

4 firm, ripe plums—peeled, destoned and chopped
8-12 cured pork loin steaks (about 1½ lb)

¼ cup red wine
1 tablespoon water
1 teaspoon sugar
¼ cup oil
freshly ground black pepper
few sprigs of parsley to garnish

Put the water, sugar and 2 tablespoons of wine into a small saucepan and heat gently until the sugar dissolves. Allow to cool. Then put into a processor with the plums and the rest of the wine and process until smooth.

Heat the oil in a large, shallow pan and sauté the steaks a few at a time for about 5-7 minutes, turning once or twice. Remove and keep hot.

Heat the plum sauce in a saucepan and spoon over the ham. Sprinkle with freshly ground black pepper, garnish with parsley sprigs and serve immediately.

Serves 4.

SALCHICHAS CON CEBOLLAS Y VINO TINTO

Sausage with Onions and Red Wine

This dish is a firm favorite with all the family. Spanish sausages are extremely good and tasty and it is important that equivalent meaty butcher's sausages are used.

8 good-sized meaty butcher's pork sausages
3 medium onions—sliced
¾ cup red wine
3-4 tablespoons oil
water
seasoning to taste

Heat the oil in a large, shallow pan and sauté the onions until soft. Add the sausages and cook gently for a few minutes more.

Pour in the red wine and allow to simmer until half the liquid is consumed. Then add enough water to just cover the sausages. Add seasoning to taste, cover and simmer gently for about 15 minutes. Remove the lid and cook vigorously for a few minutes to reduce the sauce by about a quarter.

Serve immediately, accompanied by boiled rice or creamed potatoes.

Serves 4.

CORDERO Y CABRITO / LAMB AND KID

CABRITO AL CORTIJO
Braised Kid, Country-Style

We first tasted this dish when invited to a *cortijo*, or ranch, in the Sierra Morena mountain area of Córdoba. It is a rich, full-bodied, flavorful dish which we have since often made successfully with lamb. We usually serve it with roasted red peppers or beets/beetroot in vinaigrette and boiled mint potatoes.

2 lbs boneless kid—cut into medium-sized pieces
½ cup orange juice
4 cloves garlic—sliced
2 bay leaves
½ teaspoon ground ginger
1 tablespoon lard
2 tablespoons oil
1 tablespoon all-purpose flour
2 cloves—crushed
1 cup red wine
2 teaspoons paprika
1 tablespoon chopped parsley
freshly ground black pepper
seasoning to taste

Season the meat with salt and freshly ground black pepper. Heat the oil and lard in a large, shallow casserole and quickly brown the meat all over. Sprinkle with the flour and mix well. Pour in the wine, add the garlic, stir and reduce heat.

Mix the crushed cloves, ginger and paprika with a little water and add to the casserole together with the parsley, bay leaves and orange juice. Mix thoroughly and check for seasoning. Add a little water if necessary, cover and place in a preheated, moderate oven for about 2 hours.

Serves 4.

CORDERO AL AMARILLO

Braised Lamb, Andalusian-Style

This is a luscious, mildly spicy casserole, which is equally good made with dry white wine or dry cider. It is simple to make and can be prepared in advance and reheated before serving.

2 lbs boneless lamb—cut into chunky pieces
good pinch ground saffron
3 cloves garlic—chopped
1 large onion—chopped
1 large yellow pepper—seeded and cut into strips
½ teaspoon cinnamon
2 teaspoons paprika
4-5 tablespoons oil
flour for dredging
1 tablespoon all-purpose flour
seasoning to taste
1 cup dry white wine, or sparkling dry cider
1½ cups vegetable stock
2 tablespoons chopped parsley

Dredge the meat with seasoned flour. Heat 3 tablespoons of oil in a large frying pan and quickly brown the lamb all over. Transfer the meat to a heavy casserole.

Add the remaining oil to the frying pan and sauté the chopped onions, peppers and garlic until the onions are just transparent. Then stir in the parsley. Add 1 tablespoon of all-purpose flour and mix well. Pour in the wine or cider, stirring continuously. Add the paprika, cinnamon and saffron. Then add this to the meat in the casserole, together with the stock . Season to taste, cover and place the casserole in a preheated, moderate oven for about 1½ hours.

Serve on a bed of rice, with sautéed zucchini.

Serves 4.

CHULETILLAS DE CORDERO A LA NAVARRA

Lamb Cutlets, Navarre-Style

The North of Spain produces excellent baby lamb. The cutlets are usually served *a la plancha*, or grilled, and 5-6 tiny cutlets would normally be served per person. However, for this recipe, using small white onions and green and red peppers, the cutlets would be larger and it therefore calls for about 2 per person.

8 lamb cutlets or chops
1 red pepper—seeded and chopped
1 green pepper—seeded and chopped
12-16 small white onions
4 carrots—cut into pieces
2 cloves garlic—chopped
2 stalks celery—cut into chunky pieces
1½ cups vegetable stock
3 tablespoons oil
1 bay leaf
seasoning to taste
1 tablespoon chopped parsley

1 tablespoon all-purpose flour
1 teaspoon paprika

Heat the oil in a large, heavy frying pan or casserole and lightly brown the lamb pieces. Add the peppers and garlic and sauté until soft. Stir in the flour and add the stock gradually. Then add the other vegetables, half the parsley, the spices and seasoning to taste and mix well. Cover and allow to simmer gently for about 35-40 minutes.

Sprinkle with the remaining parsley and serve. Delicious with saffron rice.

Serves 4.

GUISO DE CORDERO CON TOMATE

Lamb in Tomato Sauce

This is another of the many lamb casseroles which are so popular in Spain. In this dish the rich tomato sauce is enhanced by the use of ground pine nuts.

2 lbs boneless lamb—cut into chunky pieces
4 medium-sized ripe tomatoes—peeled and chopped
3-4 tablespoons oil
2 tablespoons pine nuts—ground
1 large onion—chopped
2 cloves garlic—chopped
1 sweet red pepper—seeded and chopped
1 tablespoon sweet basil—chopped
1 teaspoon paprika
½ cup red wine
1 cup vegetable stock
flour for dredging
seasoning to taste
water

Dredge the meat generously with seasoned flour. Heat 3 tablespoons of oil in a large, heavy frying pan or casserole and lightly brown the lamb all over. Remove the lamb.

Add the onions, red pepper and garlic to the oil in the pan and sauté until just soft (add a little more oil if necessary). Stir in the tomatoes, paprika, basil and bay leaf and allow to cook for a couple of minutes. Then stir in the ground pine nuts, the wine and stock (add a little extra water if necessary) and mix well. Check seasoning, cover and allow to simmer gently for about 1 hour, until the meat is tender.

Serves 4.

PIERNA DE CORDERO PASCUAL ASADA

Roast Leg of Spring Lamb

As mentioned earlier, baby lamb is a speciality of the North of Spain. At times the animals can be so tiny that in some restaurants, when ordering roast leg of lamb, you are served one whole leg of baby lamb per person.

1 leg baby lamb (about 3 lbs)
2 tablespoons lard
1 teaspoon wine vinegar
2 cloves garlic
seasoning to taste
2 sprigs of rosemary
water

Rub the lamb all over with the garlic and place in a roasting pan with the sprigs of rosemary. Cover the lamb with the lard and sprinkle with salt. Put in a preheated, moderate oven for about 40 minutes, basting occasionally. Then brush the lamb with the vinegar and continue cooking for an additional 20 minutes.

After cooking, some people like to mix the juices in the

pan with a little boiling water, then heat this through on top of the stove, and serve as an accompanying sauce.

Delicious with sautéed potatoes.

Serves 4.

PIERNA DE CORDERO A LA ARAGONESA

Roast Leg of Lamb, Aragonese-Style

In the Aragon region, as in some parts of France, lamb is often roasted with sliced potatoes. For many Aragonese families lamb cooked in this way still constitutes the main course of the traditional Sunday lunch.

1 leg of lamb (about 3 lbs)
1 onion—sliced
2 cloves garlic
1 tablespoon lard
10 medium potatoes
½ cup beef stock
1 tablespoon dry white wine
seasoning to taste
2 sprigs rosemary

Peel the potatoes and cut into medium-thin slices.

Rub the lamb all over with the garlic and place in the middle of a large well-greased roasting pan with the rosemary. Cover with the lard and sprinkle with salt. Arrange the potato and onion slices around the lamb and season to taste.

Mix the stock and the wine and moisten the potatoes with 4 tablespoons of the liquid. Cover with foil and place in a moderate oven for about 1 hour.

Halfway through the cooking time, remove the foil and add more stock to the potatoes if necessary. The potatoes should not be soggy. Continue cooking uncovered for the remaining time.

Serve with a green salad.

Serves 4.

RIÑONES AL JEREZ

Kidneys in Sherry Sauce

One of the most well-known Spanish dishes, *riñones al jerez,* is popular throughout the country both as a main course and as a *tapa,* or appetizer.

2 lbs lamb kidneys
2 cloves garlic—chopped
4 tablespoons oil
1 medium onion—chopped
1 tablespoon chopped parsley
1 bay leaf
seasoning to taste
2 teaspoons all-purpose flour
½ cup chicken stock
½ cup *fino,* dry sherry

Cut the kidneys in half lengthways, trim off any fat and cut into medium-sized slices. Season the kidney slices with salt and pepper. Heat the oil in a large frying pan and sauté the kidneys for about 2 minutes on both sides until lightly brown. Then remove from pan and keep hot.

Add the garlic and onion to the oil in the pan and sauté until soft. Stir in the flour and add the stock and mix well. Add the parsley, bay leaf and the sherry, bring to simmering point and cook for 3-4 minutes.

Then return the kidneys and any juices given off to the pan. Stir well. Cover and allow to cook very gently for about 3-4 minutes.

Serve on a bed of rice.
Serves 4 to 6.

TERNERA Y VACA / VEAL AND BEEF

Old Castile is renowned for its exceptional veal dishes and certainly some of the best veal we have ever tasted has been in this region, and in Avila in particular. However, the word *ternera* in Spanish is often used to refer to both veal and beef. Thus, when ordering *ternera* in a restaurant, it is well to make sure whether the dish in question is *ternera lechal* (milk-fed calf/veal) or beef.

ESCALOPE DE TERNERA A LA SEVILLANA
Veal Scallops, Seville-Style

Seville is the principal city of southern Spain, the country's major olive growing region, and the use of olives in this dish gives it a distinctive Andalusian taste.

4 veal scallops/escalopes
1 cup mushrooms—chopped
10 stuffed olives
2-3 tablespoons fresh breadcrumbs
1 tablespoon all-purpose flour
1 beaten egg
¾ cup veal or beef stock
rind of ½ lemon—cut into thin strips
3 tablespoons fresh lemon juice
2 tablespoons *oloroso* sherry
2 tablespoons light cream
1 medium onion—chopped
6 tablespoons oil
1 tablespoon chopped parsley
seasoning to taste

Put the lemon rind into a pan, add a little water and simmer for about 5 minutes until tender. Drain and set aside.

Put 3 tablespoons of oil into a large, shallow pan and sauté the onion until soft. Add the chopped mushrooms and cook for an additional 2-3 minutes. Chop 6 of the olives and add to the pan, together with the breadcrumbs. Stir in the beaten egg, seasoning to taste and mix well. Divide the mixture into 4 portions and spread one portion on each scallop. Roll up and secure with a cocktail stick.

Put the remaining oil into a frying pan and gently sauté the veal rolls until tender and lightly golden all over. Remove and keep hot.

Add the parsley to the oil in the pan and mix well. Then add the flour and stir well. Pour in the stock, lemon juice and sherry. Mix thoroughly and add the lemon rind and seasoning (if desired). Turn up the heat and cook vigorously to reduce and thicken the sauce. When the sauce begins to thicken, turn the heat to low and add the cream, stirring continuously, and allow to cook for an additional minute or so.

Spoon the sauce over the veal rolls, add one stuffed olive to the top of each roll. Serve immediately.

Serves 4.

ESCALOPE DE TERNERA A LA VALENCIANA

Veal Escalopes, Valencia-Style

This dish is a real treat and is always well received by family and friends alike. We usually serve the scallops on a bed of rice and garnish with fresh parsley. It is particularly good accompanied by a bottle of chilled dry *cava*, or sparkling wine.

8 medium-length, but very thin veal scallops/escalopes
8 wafer thin slices of *serrano*, or other cured ham

1 medium onion—finely chopped
grated rind of one orange
1 cup orange juice
3 tablespoons sunflower oil, or other light oil
3 tablespoons *fino* (bone dry) sherry
1 heaped teaspoon cornstarch/corn flour
seasoning to taste

Use one piece of ham for each veal scallop. Place the ham on top of the veal and (if necessary) flatten with a mallet. Roll the ham in the veal and fasten with a skewer or cocktail stick.

Put the oil into a large frying pan and quickly brown the scallops. Reduce the heat, add the chopped onions and sauté for a few minutes until transparent. Stir in the sherry, orange juice, rind and seasoning. Cover and simmer gently for about 20 minutes.

Remove the scallops with a perforated spoon and set aside.

Mix the cornstarch with one tablespoon of water and stir into the sauce in the pan. When sauce thickens, replace the scallops and heat through. Serve immediately.

Serves 4.

ESCALOPE DE TERNERA CON SALSA DE JEREZ Y ALMENDRAS

Veal Scallops in Sherry and Almond Sauce

A variation of the previous dish is this one we created using lemon juice, almonds and a mellow, medium-dry *amontillado* sherry.

8 medium-length, but wafer thin, scallops/escalopes
½ cup sunflower oil, or other light oil
2 tablespoons ground almonds
1 cup beef stock
3 tablespoons *amontillado* sherry

1 tablespoon lemon juice
1 cup fresh breadcrumbs
1½ tablespoons chopped parsley
6 small scallions/spring onions—washed, trimmed and finely chopped
good pinch cinnamon
seasoning to taste
lemon wedges

Mix the almonds with the stock, sherry and lemon juice and set aside.

The Stuffing:
Put 3 tablespoons of the oil into a large shallow pan and sauté the scallions until soft. Add the breadcrumbs, seasoning, cinnamon and parsley and continue cooking for a few more minutes. Remove from heat; divide this stuffing into 8 portions and place one portion on each scallop. Roll up and secure with a cocktail stick.

Wipe out the pan and add 4 tablespoons of the oil. Brown the scallops quickly in the oil, reduce heat and then pour the stock, almond and sherry mixture over the veal. Check for seasoning, cover and simmer for about 15 minutes (shaking the pan occasionally) until the scallops are cooked. Remove the lid and cook for an additional 5 minutes uncovered to thicken and reduce the sauce. Serve garnished with lemon wedges.

Serves 4.

ESCALOPE DE TERNERA CON VINO DULCE
Veal Scallops with Sweet Sherry

This is a simple, straightforward dish which we like to serve accompanied by sautéed potatoes and roasted red peppers with vinaigrette.

4 veal scallops/escalopes
¼ cup sweet *oloroso* sherry
1 tablespoon lemon juice
2 tablespoons water (optional)
2 tablespoons butter
2 tablespoons oil
freshly ground black pepper
seasoning to taste
1 tablespoon chopped tarragon
1 lemon—cut into wedges

Heat half the butter and oil in a large shallow pan and sauté 2 scallops gently until lightly golden brown—about 4 minutes on each side. Remove and keep hot. Add the remaining oil and butter to the pan and cook the other 2 scallops. Remove and keep hot. Now add the lemon juice to the pan. Pour in the sherry, water (if used), season to taste and mix well. Return the scallops to the sauce, cover and allow to cook gently for 2 minutes. Sprinkle with chopped tarragon, freshly ground black pepper and serve immediately, garnished with lemon wedges.

Serves 4.

FILETES DE SOLOMILLO CON JAMON, CHAMPIÑONES Y CEBOLLAS

Fillet Steaks with Ham, Mushrooms and Onions

This recipe from Ciudad Real in La Mancha area of Central Spain is a hearty but succulent way of cooking fillet steak. It is especially good when accompanied by a good bottle of the local Valdepeñas wine.

4 good-sized fillet steaks
3 small white onions or shallots—finely chopped
2 cups button mushrooms—washed

¼ cup (about 2 oz) chopped *serrano*, or other cured ham
¼ cup red wine
2 teaspoons chopped tarragon
¼ cup sunflower oil, or other light oil
2 tablespoons butter
seasoning to taste

Heat 3 tablespoons of oil in a large frying pan and sauté the onions until soft. Add the mushrooms, seasoning, and continue cooking for 3 minutes. Then stir in the ham and the red wine (add a little water if necessary) and cook for an additional 2 minutes.

In a heavy, shallow frying pan heat the butter and the remaining oil. Season the steaks and place in the pan. Sauté over a moderately high heat for 4-5 minutes each side or until the steaks are cooked to your liking.

Place the steaks on a serving dish, cover with the hot sauce and sprinkle with the chopped tarragon. Serve immediately.

Serves 4.

FILETES DE SOLOMILLO CON JEREZ Y MOSTAZA

Fillet Steaks with Sherry and Mustard

This dish could not be easier to make and the sauce which combines mild mustard and medium sherry gives it a wonderfully original flavor.

4 good-sized fillet steaks
2 cloves garlic—crushed
4 tablespoons *amontillado* or medium sherry
1 tablespoon butter
2 tablespoons oil
1 teaspoon prepared mild mustard
1 tablespoon chopped parsley
seasoning to taste

Heat the oil and butter in a heavy, shallow frying pan. Add the garlic and sauté until soft. Season the steaks, place in the pan and sauté over moderately high heat for 4-5 minutes each side or until the steaks are cooked to your liking. Then stir in the mustard, add the sherry and cook for about a minute. Sprinkle with chopped parsley and serve immediately.

Serves 4.

Variation:

Omit the mustard and sherry and use ½ cup red wine.

GUISO DE CARNE CON ACELGA

Beef and Celery Casserole

This dish has been a long-standing family favorite. It is ideal for a relaxing family lunch and we often prepare it a day in advance and reheat it before serving.

2 lbs stewing steak—cut into cubes
1 tablespoon lard
2 tablespoons oil
12-16 small white onions or shallots
2 carrots—peeled and diced
5 stalks celery—cut into medium-sized pieces
rind 1 orange—finely peeled and cut into strips
1 clove garlic—chopped
1 cup red wine
1 cup beef stock
1 tablespoon all-purpose flour
½ teaspoon dried mixed herbs
seasoning to taste

Put the orange rind in a small saucepan of boiling water and simmer for 5 minutes. Drain and set aside.

Heat the oil and lard in a large heavy casserole, add the meat and brown quickly. Remove the meat and set aside.

Reduce the heat, add the onions to the oil in the pan and sauté until they begin to color. Stir in the flour, then add the wine and mix well. Return the meat to the casserole. Add the herbs, garlic, stock and diced vegetables. Check for seasoning, cover and allow to simmer gently for about 1½ hours.

Stir in the orange rind 10 minutes before serving.

Serves 4.

GUISO DE CARNE GALLEGO

Braised Steak, Galician-Style

Like *pote gallego,* another typical dish from Galicia, this beef casserole also incorporates salt pork and turnips as its essential ingredients.

1½ lb braising steak—cut into medium-sized cubes
1 cup salt pork—cubed (¼ lb)
1 lb turnips—peeled and cut into medium-sized chunks
1 large onion—sliced
2 sweet red peppers—sliced
3 medium-sized ripe tomatoes—peeled and chopped
½ cup red wine
1½ cups stock
seasoning to taste
2 bay leaves
½ teaspoon oregano
2 teaspoons paprika
1 clove garlic—crushed
1 tablespoon all-purpose flour
1 tablespoon lard
2 tablespoons oil

Heat the lard and oil in a large, heavy casserole; add the meat and brown all over. Remove the meat and set aside.

Add the onion and sauté for about 2 minutes. Stir in the flour and mix well. Then add the wine and a little stock and stir until the sauce thickens.

Return the meat to the pan and pour in the remaining stock. Add the vegetables, garlic, bay leaves, oregano, paprika and seasoning to taste. Cover and place in a preheated, moderate oven for about 1½-2 hours.

Serve with boiled potatoes.

Serves 4.

GUISO DE CARNE CON PATATAS
Meat and Potato Stew

Use same ingredients as for *guiso de carne gallego* but omit the tomatoes and turnips and substitute 1½ lb of potatoes (peeled and cut into medium-sized pieces). Instead of the peppers, substitute 4 large carrots, again cut into medium-sized pieces.

Prepare as for *guiso de carne gallego,* but reserve the potatoes and add them to the stew about 30 minutes before the end of the cooking time.

REDONDO GUISADO ZARAGOZANO
Pot Roast, Saragossa-Style

Saragossa is the principal city of the Aragon region of northern Spain. In this characteristic dish from the area a little dark chocolate is used to enhance the sauce's rich wine taste.

One 4 lb piece topside or rump of beef—boned, trimmed and tied
3 large carrots—peeled and cut into slices
12-16 small white onions
3 tablespoons brandy
flour for dredging
1 tablespoon finely chopped parsley
¼ cup red wine
2 cups beef stock
1 teaspoon wine vinegar
1 tablespoon lard
2 tablespoons oil
1 teaspoon grated dark chocolate
seasoning to taste

Dredge the meat with seasoned flour.

Heat the lard and oil in a large, heavy casserole and sear or brown each side of the meat well—this should take about 10-15 minutes.

Heat the brandy in a small saucepan; pour over the beef and ignite. Add the stock, wine, vinegar, parsley, onions, carrots and seasoning. Cover tightly and allow to simmer gently for about 2½-3 hours. When cooked, remove the meat and keep hot.

Add 1 teaspoon of grated dark chocolate to the sauce, stir and simmer for about 1 minute. Carve the meat and serve with the hot sauce.

Serves 8.

RABO DE TORO
Oxtail Stew

Rabo de toro literally means bull's tail. However, whatever you call it, this rich and juicy stew cooked gently for several hours is always a mouthwatering treat, especially when served with an earthy full-flavored red wine.

2½-3 lb oxtail—cut into pieces where jointed
¼ cup (about 2 oz) chopped *serrano,* or other cured ham
2 large carrots—peeled and sliced
2 medium onions—sliced
2 cloves garlic—chopped
bouquet garni
2 cloves
¾ cup dry white wine
1 tablespoon lard
3 tablespoons oil
1 tablespoon all-purpose flour
3 cups beef stock
3 peppercorns
seasoning to taste

Heat the oil and lard in a large, heavy casserole and brown the oxtail pieces all over. Remove the oxtail pieces and set aside.

Add the ham, onions, carrots and garlic to the casserole and sauté for about 2 minutes. Pour off excess fat and add 1 tablespoon of flour to the pan and mix well. Then add the seasoning, peppercorns, cloves, bouquet garni, the oxtail pieces and enough stock (or stock and water) to cover. Bring to the boil, then reduce heat, cover tightly and allow to simmer very gently for about 3-4 hours.

Serves 4.

AVES Y CAZA

Poultry and Game

PATO / DUCK

PATO ASADO A LA ANDALUZA
Roast Duckling, Andalusian-Style

Once again, this recipe makes use of the region's famous olives to lend a robust and distinctive flavor to this Andalusian-style dish. We like to serve it with large baked potatoes.

One 4 lb duckling (approx.) or 4 duckling portions
1 cup (4 oz) button mushrooms—washed and dried
1 medium onion—chopped
2 cloves garlic—crushed
1 small can (about 6 oz) sweet red peppers
3 medium-sized ripe tomatoes—peeled and chopped
3 tablespoons *fino* (dry) sherry

3-4 tablespoons sunflower oil, or other light oil
1 tablespoon fresh parsley—chopped
16 pimento-stuffed green olives
seasoning to taste

Prepare the duckling by removing giblets, any excess fat and washing well. Then dry on a paper towel. Prick the duckling (or duckling portions) all over, sprinkle with salt and then rub the salt into the skin. Place the duckling on a wire tray inside a large roasting tin, put into a preheated, moderately hot oven and cook for 1½ hours.

Meanwhile, put the oil into a frying pan and sauté the onions and garlic until soft. Cut the red peppers into strips and add to the onions in the pan, together with the mushrooms, chopped tomatoes, parsley, olives and seasoning to taste, and cook for 10 minutes. Finally, before serving, stir in the sherry and cook for an additional 5 minutes.

If a whole duckling is used, divide it into four portions and place on a large serving dish. Cover with the sauce and serve immediately.

Serves 4.

PATO PINAR SERRANO

Duckling with Pine Nuts, Limes and Grapes—A House Speciality

Our home in Spain is situated in the middle of a pine wood and nestles among some of the tallest and most majestic pines, many of which must be around 15-20 metres tall (though we have never measured them). The pines tower above our two-story house. We are therefore fortunate enough to be able to collect our own pine nuts. And, in the early autumn, when the local grapes are sweet and plentiful and the pinecones are gathered for their fruit, the tiny nuts or piñones, the following dish comes into its own.

We created this dish several years ago when we moved

into our new home in Spain. We enjoyed it so much that it now is featured regularly on our menu.

This dish is also ideal for a dinner party, as it can be cooked in advance and reheated—in this case the grapes should be added during the reheating stage, some 5 minutes before serving.

One 4 lb duckling (approx.) or 4 duckling portions
½ cup red wine
1 cup chicken stock
2 tablespoons brandy
pinch ground saffron
1 tablespoon fresh parsley—chopped
¼ cup pine nuts
rind of one whole medium lime—grated
juice of ½ medium lime
1 clove garlic—finely chopped
1 bay leaf
about 6 small scallions/spring onions—washed, trimmed and chopped
½ teaspoon chopped tarragon
1 level tablespoon all-purpose flour
3 tablespoons sunflower oil
12-16 plump, sweet grapes
seasoning to taste

If a whole duckling is used, first cut into quarters and remove excess fat. Wash the meat and dry on a paper towel. Then prick the duckling skin all over.

Combine the chopped parsley, pine nuts and saffron and set aside.

Put the oil into a large, heavy casserole or frying pan and sauté the duckling portions until golden brown all over. Pour over the brandy and set alight and, when the flame subsides, remove the duckling portions and set aside.

Add the scallions, garlic, tarragon and bay leaf to the pan

and sauté for 3-4 minutes. Stir in the flour and slowly pour in the wine, stock, lime juice, rind and seasoning to taste. Add the duckling portions, cover and simmer gently for about one hour, shaking the pan from time to time. Then stir in the saffron, pine nuts and parsley mixture (add a little water if necessary) and cook for an additional 20 minutes.

Halve and seed the grapes and, about 5 minutes before serving, stir them into the casserole.

Serves 4.

Variations:

Use this recipe, but substitute 2 spring chickens for the duckling (half a spring chicken per person), for a very tasty dish. When using spring chicken, the cooking time should be reduced. Instead of simmering for one hour in the first instance, simmer for 35 minutes, and when adding the nuts, etc., cook for an additional 10 minutes. Add the grapes 5 minutes before serving.

If pine nuts are not available, use toasted sliced almonds instead.

PATO SILVESTRE CON SALSA DE PEPINO Y FRAMBUESA

Roast Wild Duck with Cucumber and Raspberry Sauce

We make this dish as our special treat whenever we are able to get a mallard. The cucumber and raspberry sauce complements the somewhat drier but rich meat of the wild duck. We often prepare the sauce in large quatities and freeze it for later use.

2 mallard ducks weighing about 1¼ lbs each
4 tablespoons butter
seasoning to taste

The Sauce:

1 large cucumber—peeled and cut into chunks

3 tablespoons wine vinegar
1 cup raspberries (scant ¼ lb)
1 tablespoon sugar
1 generous cup chicken stock
2 teaspoons arrowroot
juice of half lime
2 teaspoons honey
1 tablespoon light cream

To cook the mallard:

Wash the mallard well and dry on paper towels. Do not prick the skin. Put a nut of butter inside each duck and use the rest of the butter to coat the skin. Sprinkle with salt and put into a preheated, moderately hot oven for about 35 minutes until cooked.

To make the sauce:

Put the cucumber into a pan with salted boiling water, cover and simmer for about 10-15 minutes. Then drain and press the cucumber through a sieve with a wooden spoon or process to produce a smooth purée. Set aside.

Put the vinegar into a saucepan, add the sugar and bring to the boil. Allow the sugar to dissolve and cook until the liquid becomes syrupy. Pour in the stock and simmer uncovered until the liquid has reduced by about half.

Add the cucumber purée and stir well. Mix the arrowroot with the lime juice and 2 tablespoons of cold water. Pour this slowly into the sauce, stirring constantly. Bring the sauce to the boil again and stir in the raspberries, seasoning and the honey. Simmer for an additional 2 minutes. Finally, fold in the cream.

Remove the mallard from the oven, cut in half and serve with the hot sauce.

Serves 4.

GALLINA, POLLO Y PAVO / CHICKEN AND TURKEY

GALLINA EN PEPITORIA

Chicken "Hodgepodge" with Almonds

This casserole is a speciality of Valladolid in Old Castile. It is a rich, tasty dish and one we always order when it appears on a local menu.

1 medium roasting chicken (about 3 lbs)—cut into pieces
5 tablespoons oil
1 onion—chopped
1 clove garlic—crushed
1 tablespoon parsley—finely chopped
2 tablespoons ground almonds
1 tablespoon pine nuts—ground
1 bay leaf
pinch of ground saffron
1 cup dry white wine
flour for dredging
yolks of 2 hard-boiled eggs
seasoning to taste
water

Coat the chicken pieces in seasoned flour.

Heat the oil in a large, shallow pan and quickly brown the chicken pieces all over. Reduce heat, add the chopped onion and bay leaf to the oil and sauté until soft. Pour in the wine; cover and allow to cook gently for about 30 minutes.

Meanwhile, mix together the garlic, ground pine nuts, almonds, saffron, parsley and salt to taste and stir well to form a paste.

Stir the paste into the casserole, add sufficient water just to cover the chicken and cook gently for an additional 30 minutes.

Just before serving, mash the egg yolks with the back of a spoon or fork and stir into the casserole. Turn up the heat and, stirring gently, allow to cook for a few more minutes uncovered until the sauce thickens.

Serve with triangles of fried bread.

Serves 4-6.

PECHUGAS DE POLLO EMPANADAS

Chicken Breasts in Breadcrumbs

Fried chicken breasts in breadcrumbs is a regular feature on the tables of most Spanish households. It is normally served with fried potatoes and a green salad.

4 good-sized chicken breast portions—skinned and cut in half lengthwise
2 lemons
1 tablespoon fresh parsley—chopped
seasoning to taste
1½ cups dry, fine breadcrumbs
1 cup oil for frying
1 large beaten egg

Squeeze the lemons.

Place the chicken breasts on a large plate and pour the lemon juice over them, sprinkle with parsley and season to taste. Allow to marinate for about 2 hours.

Then dip the breasts in the the beaten egg and coat with breadcrumbs.

Heat the oil in a large, shallow pan and fry the chicken over a moderate heat, turning once, until lightly golden on both sides.

Serves 4.

PECHUGAS DE POLLO EN SALSA DE NARANJA Y YERBABUENA

Chicken Breasts in Orange and Mint Sauce

This dish is from Murcia, the region which lies between Andalusia and Valencia. The combination of mint and orange juice in this recipe highlights its Moorish origin and lends something of an exotic flavor to what might otherwise be a routine dish.

4 chicken breast portions—skinned
2 tablespoons oil
1 tablespoon butter
¾ cup orange juice
rind of 1 orange
juice of ½ lemon
1 tablespoon fresh mint—chopped
seasoning to taste

Peel the orange rind thinly and cut into fine shreds. Put into a small pan of boiling water and allow to simmer for about 5 minutes. Then strain, rinse with cold water and set aside.

Season the chicken breasts. Put the oil and butter into a large, shallow pan and heat. Add the breasts and sauté for a few minutes on each side until lightly golden.

Add the lemon juice, orange juice and rind, cover and allow to cook gently for another 10-15 minutes.

Just before serving, add the mint, stir for a few seconds and transfer to a serving dish.

Serves 4.

POLLO AL AJILLO
Garlic Chicken

Pollo al ajillo is an Andalusian dish which is now popular all over Spain. It is simple to make and delicious with potatoes or rice salad.

1 plump roasting chicken (about 3½ lb)—cut into pieces
½ cup oil
5 cloves garlic—coarsely chopped
seasoning to taste

Put the oil in a large, shallow pan and heat. Season the chicken pieces and fry in the oil until golden all over. Add the garlic and stir well. Lower heat and allow the chicken and garlic to cook for about 20 minutes, stirring occasionally. Then cover the pan and allow to cook for an additional 15 minutes.

Remove the chicken pieces from the pan, drain on a paper towel and serve immediately.

Serves 4-5.

POLLO A LA CHILINDRÓN
Aragonese-Style Chicken

Pollo a la chilindrón is one of the many dishes which use sweet red peppers, tomatoes, ham and onions to make a rich pungent sauce. The dish should be served with lots of crusty bread to mop up the delicious sauce.

1 plump roasting chicken (about 3½ lb)—cut into 8 pieces
4 tablespoons olive oil
1 large onion—coarsely chopped
2 cloves garlic—chopped
2-3 sweet red peppers—seeded and chopped

4 medium-sized ripe tomatoes—peeled and chopped
¼ cup (about 2 oz) chopped *serrano* ham, or substitute
a few green olives—pitted
a few black olives—pitted
seasoning to taste

Put the oil into a large, shallow frying pan. Season the chicken portions, add them to the pan and sauté until golden. Transfer the chicken pieces to a heavy, flameproof casserole and set aside.

Add the peppers, onion, garlic and ham to the oil remaining in the pan, mix well and sauté until soft. Stir in the tomatoes, season to taste and cook for about 5 minutes over a moderate heat.

When the vegetables are well blended, add the mixture to the chicken pieces in the casserole and mix thoroughly. Cover and allow to simmer gently for about 35 minutes until tender. Finally, add the olives and serve.

Serves 4.

POLLO OVETENSE

Chicken Breasts, Asturian-Style

The word *ovetense* means from Oviedo, which is the principal city of Asturias. This is a simple chicken dish from this cider region of northern Spain. Like many other such dishes, it can be made in advance and reheated, adding the cream, grapes and croutons before serving.

4 chicken breast portions—skinned
flour for dredging
2 tablespoons butter
2 tablespoons sunflower oil, or other light oil
1 medium onion—chopped
1 clove garlic—chopped (optional)

1 cup cider
1 tablespoon chopped parsley
2 tablespoons *migas* or croutons
12 grapes—deseeded and halved
2 tablespoons light cream
3 teaspoons paprika
seasoning to taste

Dredge the chicken breasts generously with seasoned flour.

Heat the oil and butter in a large, shallow pan and sauté the chicken until lightly brown all over. Remove the chicken and keep warm.

Add the onion and garlic to the pan and cook until soft. Stir in the parsley, paprika and seasoning to taste. Then pour in the cider, bring to the boil, stirring gently and add a little water if necessary. Lower heat and return the chicken to the casserole. Cover and allow to simmer gently for about 10-15 minutes. Turn heat to very low (do not allow to boil) and stir in the cream, grapes and croutons. Serve immediately.

Serves 4.

PAVO CON ESPARRAGOS, JAMON Y CASTAÑAS

Turkey with Asparagus, Ham and Chestnuts

We first created this recipe several years ago for a special celebration dinner. The combination of cured ham, asparagus and chestnuts turns this turkey dish into a hit with family and friends alike.

12-16 chestnuts (or frozen/canned prepared chestnuts)
4 good-sized turkey breast fillets (approx. 1¼ lbs)
4 asparagus spears—cooked

¼ cup (about 2 oz) diced *serrano*, or other cured ham
2 teaspoons chopped tarragon
1 tablespoon chopped parsley
6 scallions/spring onions—chopped
1 clove garlic—finely chopped
½ cup dry wine
1½ cups chicken stock
1 tablespoon butter
3 tablespoons oil
1 tablespoon all-purpose flour
freshly ground black pepper
flour for dredging
seasoning to taste

To prepare fresh chestnuts:

Put the nuts in cold water and bring to the boil. Allow to simmer for about 1 minute, then remove from heat. Lift the chestnuts out of the water one at a time and peel away both the outer and inner skins. Simmer the peeled chestnuts in water for about 15 minutes.

Preparing fresh chestnuts can be quite laborious and frozen chestnuts are equally good and only need to be cooked in boiling water for a few minutes until tender.

To cook the turkey:

Dredge the turkey breast fillets with seasoned flour, then shake off excess. Heat the oil in a large, heavy casserole and lightly brown the fillets all over for about 2 minutes. Remove the fillets and set aside.

Add the scallions and garlic to the oil in the casserole and sauté until soft. Add the ham and stir in 1 tablespoon of flour. Pour in the wine and mix well. Then add the stock, parsley, salt to taste and freshly ground black pepper (if necessary, add a little water). Return the turkey fillets to the casserole, cover and place in a preheated, moderately hot oven for 20 minutes.

Serve on a bed of rice, garnished with asparagus spears, chopped tarragon and the hot chestnuts.
Serves 4.

PAVO EN SALSA DE MACEDONIA AL HORNO

Braised Turkey Breasts Macedonia

This is a very original and delicately flavored dish combining turkey breasts, apples, pears and plums. The recipe is equally successful with pork—substitute 4 large pork chops for the turkey breasts.

1½ lb turkey breast—cut into slices
1 medium onion—chopped
good pinch ground ginger
1 bay leaf
1 small eating apple—peeled, cored and sliced
1 small firm but sweet pear—peeled, cored and sliced
2 ripe but firm plums—quartered and stoned
juice ½ lemon
1 teaspoon clear honey
2 tablespoons butter
2 tablespoons oil
freshly ground black pepper
¾ cup dry white wine
flour for dredging
1 cup chicken stock
1 teaspoon paprika
1 tablespoon green coriander—chopped
1 teaspoon arrowroot
seasoning to taste

Dredge the turkey slices with seasoned flour.
Heat the oil and butter in a heavy casserole and lightly

brown the turkey breast slices on both sides. Remove and set aside.

Add the onions to the pan and sauté until soft. Add the bay leaf, half the coriander, paprika and ginger and stir well. Return the turkey to the casserole and pour in the stock and wine. Check for seasoning, cover and place in a preheated, moderate oven for about 15 minutes. Then add the plums, apple and pear slices, honey and lemon juice to the casserole. Mix the arrowroot with a little cold water and stir into the casserole. Cover and continue cooking for an additional 25 minutes until the turkey is tender and the fruit soft.

Serve on a bed of rice and sprinkle with a little green coriander.

Serves 4.

CODORNICES, PERDICES Y PICHONES / QUAIL, PARTRIDGE AND PIGEON

CODORNICES ASADAS
Roast Quail

Quail are plentiful throughout Spain. We were first served this dish in a small family inn in Extremadura and we have since had *codornices* in many other country restaurants in Andalusia, New Castile and the Basque country—all equally good.

8 oven-ready quail
8 thin slices fatty bacon
8 grape vine leaves (optional)
8 slices bread for frying
2 tablespoons lard
oil for frying
seasoning to taste
fresh parsley or watercress to garnish
lemon wedges

Season the birds inside and out.

Divide the lard into 8 portions. Spread one portion on each grape leaf. Press this over each quail breast. (If you are not using the grape leaves, apply the lard directly to the quail breasts.) Wrap a slice of bacon around each bird and tie with string. Put into a roasting pan and place in a preheated, moderate oven for about 20 minutes.

Before serving, cover the bottom of a frying pan with oil and quickly fry a slice of bread on both sides until golden, then continue with the remaining bread, adding oil as required.

When the quail are cooked, remove the grape leaves and bacon and place each bird on top of a slice of fried bread. Garnish with fresh parsley or watercress and lemon wedges and serve immediately.

Serves 4 as a main course.

CODORNICES EN PIMIENTOS

Quail in Pepper Nests

When served at a dinner party this dish always brings a gasp of delight from guests—it seems to stimulate both conversation and appetite.

8 oven ready quail
8 large green peppers—stems removed and seeded
4 medium-sized ripe tomatoes—peeled and chopped
1 large onion—chopped
1 clove garlic—chopped
1 tablespoon fresh parsley—chopped
8 thin slices fatty bacon
4 tablespoons *migas* or croutons
4 tablespoons oil
1 cup chicken stock
seasoning

Sprinkle the quail with salt.

Heat 4 tablespoons of oil in a large frying pan and lightly brown the quail all over. Remove from the pan and set aside.

Add the onions, garlic and parsley to the oil in the pan and sauté until soft. Stir in the tomatoes, stock and seasoning to taste and cook 3-4 minutes. Pour the sauce into a heavy casserole.

Wrap a slice of thin fatty bacon around each bird. Insert one bird into each green pepper. Place the peppers upright in the casserole, on top of the sauce, and bake in a preheated, moderately hot oven for about 35-40 minutes until tender.

Place the nests in a seving dish and pour the sauce over. Serve with hot croutons or *migas*.

Serves 4 as a main course.

PERDICES ESTOFADAS
Stewed Partridge

This is a luscious dish which is ideal for a special lunch or light dinner. We like to serve it with roast potatoes and artichoke hearts.

4 small partridges
¼ cup (about 2 oz) chopped *serrano*, or other cured ham
3-4 tablespoons sunflower oil, or other light oil
3 carrots—cut into medium-length pieces
12 small white onions—peeled
2½ cups (about lO oz) mushrooms—thickly sliced
2 tablespoons brandy
1½ tablespoons fresh tarragon—chopped
¾ cup red wine
1 cup chicken stock
2 teaspoons cornstarch/corn flour

1 bay leaf
seasoning to taste

Clean the partridges and season inside and out.

Heat the oil in a large flameproof casserole and gently brown the partridges all over.

Warm the brandy, pour it over the birds and ignite. When the flame subsides, add the onions and sauté for a few minutes. Add the ham and cook for an additional 2 minutes. Then stir in the mushrooms, carrots, bay leaf, seasoning to taste and half the tarragon; mix well and add the wine and stock. Cover and simmer gently for about 45-50 minutes.

When tender, transfer the partridges to a serving dish and keep hot.

Mix the cornstarch with a little water and add to the sauce in the casserole; simmer gently and stir until the sauce thickens. Then pour over the partridges. Sprinkle with the remaining tarragon and serve.

Serves 4.

PERDICES CON SALSA DE PEPINO Y NARANJA

Roast Partidge with Cucumber and Orange Sauce

The rich dark meat of the partridge marries beautifully with the cucumber and orange sauce—the secret of which lies in the addition of the orange flavored liqueur just before serving.

For the Birds:

4 small (or 2 large) partridges
4 tablespoons butter
1 cup red wine
4 thin slices fatty bacon
flour for dredging
seasoning to taste

For the Sauce:

1 large cucumber
1 tablespoon red currant jelly
juice of 1 orange
rind of ½ orange
juice of ½ lime
1½ teaspoons arrowroot
1 tablespoon *oloroso* sherry
1 tablespoon Spanish *licor 43*, or other orange-flavored liqueur like Grand Marnier
6 tablespoons chicken stock
1 small nut butter
1 tablespoon light cream

Season the partridges inside and out. Put a nut of butter inside each bird and spread the rest of the butter over the carcass. Place a slice of bacon over each breast. Put the birds into a roasting pan and place in a preheated hot oven for about 15 minutes. Then pour the wine over the birds and baste well. Reduce the oven temperature to moderate and allow the partridges to cook for another 30 minutes, basting occasionally. Remove the bacon, dredge the birds lightly with flour, baste again and return to the oven for an additional 10 minutes.

Make the sauce:

Peel the cucumber and cut into chunks. Put into a pan with salted boiling water and simmer for about 10 minutes. Drain and then press the cucumber through a sieve with a wooden spoon. Set aside.

Peel the rind of 1 orange and ½ lime very thinly and cut into shreds. Put into a pan with boiling water and simmer for 5 minutes. Then drain, rinse the rind in cold water and set aside.

Strain the juice of 1 orange and ½ lime. Then put the red currant jelly into a pan; add the strained juices, seasoning and stock, and simmer gently for 2 minutes. Stir in the cucumber purée and sherry. Mix the arrowroot with a little cold water and add to the sauce, together with the butter and cream. Stir constantly until the sauce thickens. Remove from heat and stir in the orange liqueur and the prepared rind just before serving.

Serves 4.

PERDICES CON SIDRA Y UVAS

Partridge with Cider and Grapes

This is another excellent and delicately flavored dish from Asturias in the north of Spain.

4 small partridges
1 cup ripe sweet grapes—peeled and seeded
1 tablespoon butter
3 tablespoons oil
flour for dredging
1½ cups cider
1½ teaspoons cornstarch/corn flour
seasoning to taste

Dredge the partridges with seasoned flour.

Heat the oil and butter in a large frying pan and lightly brown the birds all over. Transfer to a large, heavy casserole. Pour the fat from the pan over the birds, add the cider and adjust seasoning. Cover and place in a preheated, moderately hot oven for about 45 minutes.

About 15 minutes before serving, mix the cornstarch with a little cold water and add to the casserole, together with the grapes, and stir well.

Serves 4.

Variation:

Stoned cherries may be used instead of the grapes.

PICHONES ESTOFADOS

Braised Pigeon

This dish is from the Navarre region, at the foot of the Pyrenees, in northern Spain. The dark strong game meat marries beautifully with the rich dark chocolate sauce and small white onions.

4 small pigeons/squabs
12 small white onions
2 cloves garlic—chopped
½ cup dry white wine
1¼ cups chicken stock
1½ teaspoons grated dark chocolate
1 level tablespoon all-purpose flour
3 tablespoons oil
1 tablespoon lard
1 bay leaf
flour for dredging
seasoning to taste
lemon wedges
few sprigs parsley or watercress

Dredge the birds with seasoned flour.

Heat the lard and oil in a large, heavy casserole and lightly brown the birds all over. Remove the birds from the pan. Add the onions and garlic to the fat in the pan and cook for a few minutes.

Stir in one tablespoon of flour and mix well. Add the wine, stock, bay leaf and seasoning to taste and stir over a moderately high heat until the sauce thickens. Remove from the heat and stir in the chocolate. Return the pigeons to the pan, basting them with the well-mixed sauce. Cover and place the casserole in a preheated, moderate oven for about 1 hour, until the birds are tender.

Serve garnished with lemon wedges and parsley or watercress.

Serves 4.

CONEJO / RABBIT

GUISO DE CONEJO CON ACEITUNAS

Rabbit Casserole with Olives

It is usually a good idea to marinate rabbit for at least 12 hours, as this helps to tenderize the meat as well as giving it a delicate flavor.

We will never forget the wonderful combination of garlic, coriander, almonds and olives when we first tasted this dish at the home of a friend in Leon in the Northwest of Spain.

1 young rabbit (approx. 2½ lbs)—cut into pieces
3 teaspoons vinegar
4 cups water
1 tablespoon lard
2 tablespoons oil
2 cloves garlic—chopped
2 medium onions—chopped
1 tablespoon ground blanched almonds
1½ cups (about 6 oz) button mushrooms
small jar (3 oz size) pitted green olives—halved
1 tablespoon green coriander—chopped
2 cloves
1 bay leaf
1 cup red wine
¾ cup white stock
flour for dredging
seasoning to taste

Put the water and vinegar into a large dish, add the rabbit

pieces and allow to marinate overnight. Then remove and dry on a paper towel.

Dredge the rabbit pieces in seasoned flour.

Heat the oil and lard in a large, heavy casserole and lightly brown the rabbit all over. Remove the rabbit and add the chopped onions, bay leaf and garlic to the fat in the pan and sauté until soft.

Add the cloves, wine, stock and seasoning to taste. Mix well, cover and allow to simmer gently for about 1 hour.

About 15 minutes before serving, remove the lid, stir in the ground almonds, olives and mushrooms and allow the sauce to thicken.

Serve with rice and garnish with coriander.

Serves 4.

SALSAS

Sauces

SALSA DE ALMENDRAS (1)

Almond Sauce (1)

Salsa de almendras is popular throughout Spain as an accompaniment to hard-boiled eggs, boiled chicken, cold meats and fish.

yolks of 2 hard-boiled eggs
½ cup ground almonds (approx. 2 oz)
2 cups milk
freshly ground black pepper
salt to taste

Blend the almonds and egg yolks in a mortar or bowl to make a smooth paste. Add the milk slowly, mixing well. Season to taste. Put the sauce into a saucepan and simmer over a medium heat to thicken and reduce the sauce to a rich, creamy consistency.

Makes about 1½ cups sauce.

SALSA DE ALMENDRAS (2)

Almond Sauce (2)

This is another slightly richer but delicious almond sauce which is very good with turkey and chicken dishes.

½ cup blanched almonds—finely chopped
1 cup chicken stock
2 teaspoons all-purpose flour
1 tablespoon butter
seasoning to taste
pinch ground mace
½ teaspoon ground paprika
few drops lemon or lime juice
1 tablespoon light cream
1 tablespoon *amontillado* sherry (optional)

Put the butter into a shallow frying pan and slowly brown the almonds.

Remove pan from heat and stir in the flour, then add the stock and stir constantly until boiling point is reached. Add the seasoning, mace and paprika. Reduce heat and simmer for about 5 minutes until the sauce has a creamy consistency. Stir in the lemon/lime juice, the cream and sherry (if used), and continue cooking for 2-3 minutes more.

Makes about 1 cup sauce.

SALSA BECHAMEL

White Sauce

This is a basic white sauce used as an accompaniment to innumerable dishes and as the basis for other sauces.

1 tablespoon butter
1 tablespoon all-purpose flour

1 cup hot milk
2 peppercorns
1 bay leaf
seasoning to taste

Put the milk into a saucepan, add the peppercorns, bay leaf and seasoning, and heat gently.

Meanwhile, melt the butter in a saucepan, then remove from heat and add the flour, mix well to form a paste. Strain the hot milk through a sieve.

Return the pan with the paste to the heat and gradually pour the strained milk over the paste, stirring constantly. Allow to cook over a low heat until the sauce thickens.

Makes about 1 cup sauce.

SALSA DE CHAMPIÑONES
Mushroom Sauce

Salsa de champiñones is a good general-purpose sauce, particularly popular served with white fish, vegetables and chicken dishes.

1 cup of white sauce (see *salsa bechamel*)
1 cup button mushrooms
1 tablespoon butter
seasoning to taste
pinch cayenne pepper
pinch ground nutmeg
1 tablespoon light cream

Wash, trim and chop the mushrooms. Prepare the hot white sauce as indicated in previous recipe.

Put the butter into a frying pan and sauté the mushrooms for 2-3 minutes. Add the seasoning, nutmeg and cayenne pepper and mix well. Stir the mushroom mixture into the white sauce, add the cream and simmer gently for about 2 minutes.

Makes about 1½ cups sauce.

MAYONESA / MAYONNAISE

SALSA MAYONESA

Mayonnaise

When making mayonnaise take care that the ingredients are not too cold and, if the eggs are kept in the refrigerator, take them out at least an hour before use.

2 egg yolks
2 tablespoons white wine vinegar or lemon juice
½ teaspoon Dijon-type mustard
salt to taste
1 cup olive oil
ground white pepper

Place the egg yolks in a bowl with the mustard, salt and pepper, and beat with a sauce whisk for a minute or so. When the mixture is creamy, add the oil: at first add the oil drop by drop (making sure that each drop of oil has been absorbed before adding the next), then the remaining oil may be added in a slow stream, beating constantly until the mixture starts to become thick. Now slowly beat in the lemon juice or vinegar.

Makes about 1 cup sauce.

ALI OLI

Garlic Mayonnaise

There are many regional versions of, and names for, *ali oli* (meaning garlic oil). This, I suppose, is not surprising given the length of time the sauce has been around. In medieval Spain it was called *ajolio* and was thought to have been brought to the Iberian Peninsula by the Romans. It was also known as *aillouse* in France during the Middle Ages and is still considered to be a speciality of the Provence region, where it is called *aïoli*. In Spain it is known variously as *ajiaceite, ajoaceite* and, more commonly nowadays, as *ali oli*.

2 egg yolks
8 cloves garlic
2 teaspoons lemon juice
good pinch of salt
1 generous cup olive oil

Before making *ali oli*, make sure the oil is of room temperature or it will not blend properly.

Crush the garlic cloves in a mortar, add the salt and lemon juice and mix to a smooth paste. Transfer to a large bowl. Beat the egg yolks and stir into the garlic paste. Then, stirring constantly and preferably in the same direction, mix in the olive oil drop by drop. Continue until the mayonnaise has a thick, creamy consistency. If you find that it becomes too thick, it may be thinned by adding a teaspoon of lukewarm water from time to time. The final result should be a creamy, pale yellow mayonnaise which is a wonderful accompaniment to fish, shellfish and light meat.

Makes about 1 cup sauce.

Note:

Should you find, during preparation, that the oil comes back to the surface, or that the mayonnaise curdles, this is often remedied by taking the following steps:

Crush another clove of garlic and a pinch of salt in a mortar, add one beaten egg yolk and one teaspoon of lukewarm water. Pour this into a bowl and, beating constantly, start to incorporate the original *ali oli* a teaspoon at a time.

MAYONESA VERDE (1)
Green Mayonnaise (1)

This is delicious with salmon, trout or cold white fish.

1 cup mayonnaise (see p. 208), or use prepared mayonnaise
large handful parsley
2 sprigs chervil
2 sprigs tarragon
3 spinach leaves
1 tablespoon light cream
seasoning to taste
1½ cups boiling water

Put the spinach and herbs into a saucepan, add boiling, salted water, cover and simmer for about 10 minutes. Drain and then press the spinach and herbs through a sieve (to give about one tablespoon of green purée) and allow to cool. Just before serving, add the purée to the mayonnaise, stir in the cream and season to taste.

Makes about 1 cup sauce.

MAYONESA VERDE (2)
Green Mayonnaise (2)

This is our favorite recipe for green mayonnaise. It makes a deliciously light and slightly piquant sauce, which is an excellent accompaniment to vegetables, fish and cold shellfish.

½ cup fresh mayonnaise, or use prepared mayonnaise
1 (large) egg white
2 tablespoons finely chopped parsley
2 tablespoons minced scallions/spring onions

2 teaspoons lemon juice
1 teaspoon mild, tarragon-flavored, mustard
seasoning to taste

Whisk the egg white until stiff and set aside.

Crush the parsley in a mortar, then transfer to a mixing bowl. Add the mayonnaise, scallions, mustard, lemon juice and seasoning to taste, and mix well. Gently fold in the beaten egg white, and combine thoroughly.

Makes about 1 cup.

MAYONESA VERDE (3)

Green Mayonnaise (3)

This is a simplified, quick version of the previous two recipes.

1 cup mayonnaise
2 tablespoons finely chopped parsley
1 tablespoon minced scallions/spring onions
2 tablespoons finely chopped cucumber
a few chopped capers
2 drops green food coloring
seasoning to taste

Combine all the ingredients and mix well.

Makes about 1 cup.

ROMESCU

Pepper and Almond Sauce

Romescu is a cold sauce from the Tarragon area of Catalonia. It is usually served with cold shellfish or cold white meats. *Romescu* is often mixed with the garlic mayonnaise *ali oli* (in proportions to suit individual taste). There are many different strengths of *romescu,* from the very mild, to the comparatively hot versions, but in most families and restaurants, a balance is struck and a medium-hot *romescu* is usually offered.

¼ cup ground, blanched almonds (about 1 oz)
2 tablespoons red-wine vinegar
2 cloves garlic—chopped
1 large (2 small) ripe tomato—peeled and chopped
good pinch cayenne pepper
good pinch salt (or to taste)
¾ cup olive oil
1 tablespoon of fried breadcrumbs

Put the garlic, almonds, cayenne pepper, salt and fried breadcrumbs in a large bowl and crush with the back of a wooden spoon. Stir in the vinegar and tomatoes and mash well to form a smooth paste. (Alternatively, put all the above ingredients into an electric blender and process until just smooth.)

Then beat in the oil, a little at a time, with a rotary beater—making sure that the oil has been completely absorbed before adding more. When half the oil has been added, pour in the rest in a slow stream, beating constantly. Season to taste. The finished sauce should resemble a thick, reddish-brown cream. (If you find the sauce is too thick, it may be thinned by stirring in a little of the stock or juices from the cooked fish or meat.)

Makes generous cup of sauce.

SALSA DE TOMATE
Tomato Sauce

Salsa de tomate is used in innumerable dishes in Spain. It is also very popular as an accompaniment to hot or cold

Spanish omelet, croquettes, and many rice and vegetable dishes.

3 tablespoons olive oil
4 large ripe tomatoes—peeled and chopped (or one 16 oz can chopped tomatoes)
1 medium onion—finely chopped
½ teaspoon oregano
pinch of salt
½ teaspoon sugar (optional)

Put the oil into a large frying pan, add the chopped onion and sauté until soft. Add the chopped tomatoes and oregano and simmer for about 10-15 minutes. Then pass the mixture through a fine sieve and mix in the salt and sugar (if used).

Reheat before serving.

Makes about 2 cups sauce.

SALSA VERDE (1)

Green Sauce (1)

This smooth green sauce is delicious with hard-boiled eggs, poached fish, or chicken dishes.

1 cup of white sauce as indicated on p. 206.
3 spinach leaves
2 sprigs tarragon
2 sprigs chervil
2 sprigs chives
2 sprigs parsley
1½ cups boiling water
seasoning to taste

Put the spinach and herbs into a large pan with the boiling water and salt to taste, cover and simmer for about

10 minutes. Drain and then press the spinach and herbs through a sieve to give about 1 tablespoon of green purée. Add the green purée to the hot white sauce, season to taste and mix well.

This sauce should be light green in color.

Makes about 1 cup sauce.

SALSA VERDE (2)

Green (Parsley) Sauce (2)

Dry white wine is very often used to make parsley sauce in Spain. However, this recipe for parsley sauce includes garlic, ground ginger and, as we prefer it, sparkling dry cider—which gives a slightly more piquant flavor.

Parsley sauce is very popular throughout Spain with rabbit, chicken and many vegetables.

2 cloves garlic
¼ cup olive oil
¼ cup finely chopped parsley
salt to taste
2 tablespoons all-purpose flour
½ teaspoon powdered ginger
scant ½ cup water
1 cup sparkling dry cider
freshly ground black pepper
3 tablespoons light cream

Put the oil into a large, shallow, frying pan and sauté the whole garlic cloves until golden brown, then remove the garlic.

In a mortar (or electric processor), crush the garlic and parsley to a paste, add the salt, ginger, pepper and flour and mix well. Add this mixture to the oil still in the pan and stir well over a moderate heat. Slowly add the cider, stirring constantly as the sauce simmers and thickens. Then add the water, continue stirring and allow to simmer for 2-3 minutes. Finally, turn the heat to low, fold in the cream and cook for an additional couple of minutes.

Serve with shellfish, vegetables or light meat.

Makes about 1½ cups of sauce.

SALSA VINAGRETA SENCILLA

Basic Vinaigrette Sauce

3 tablespoons olive oil
1 tablespoon wine vinegar
good pinch salt
freshly ground black pepper

Combine all the ingredients and mix well.

Makes scant ¼ cup sauce.

SALSA VINAGRETA (2)

Vinaigrette Sauce (2)

This is very good as a dressing for freshly cooked vegetables, salads and fish dishes.

3 tablespoons olive oil
1 tablespoon wine vinegar
good pinch salt
freshly ground black pepper
2 slices of onion
1 teaspoon chopped parsley

Put the onion, salt, oil and parsley into a bowl and allow to stand for about 30 minutes. Then remove the onion and discard. Stir in the vinegar and the freshly ground black pepper and mix well.

Makes scant ¼ cup sauce.

POSTRES Y PASTELES

Desserts, Cakes, Pastries

Most Spaniards are brought up on desserts which consist mainly of some form of fresh fruit; cakes and pastries usually are reserved for *merienda*, or tea time. Restaurants also offer a fairly limited dessert menu which invariably includes fruit, the ubiquitous caramel custard, or a variety of ice creams and ice cream tarts. However, the desserts that are most common are ones made with eggs and sugar, usually in the form of rich custards, meringues and mousse, as well as those made with batter. For us, perhaps the most delicious are the desserts which combine a creamy custard with either batter, as in cream fritters, or with a light meringue, as in coffee pudding.

ARROZ CON LECHE

Spanish-Style Rice Pudding

Most households have their own special recipe for rice pudding, but in most cases in Spain the pudding is cooked in a saucepan on top of the stove rather than in the oven, and incorporates a beaten egg yolk to give a rich and creamy result. This is one of our favorite recipes for *arroz con leche.*

generous ¼ cup short-grain rice
¼ cup sugar (or more, to taste)
rind of 1 lemon—cut into long strips
3 cups milk
2 teaspoons butter
1 egg yolk—beaten
3 cups water
ground cinnamon to decorate

Mix the beaten egg yolk with 2 tablespoons of cold milk and set aside.

Put the rice in a saucepan with the water. When it starts to boil, lower heat and allow to cook for 10 minutes. Then transfer to a sieve and drain off the water. Put the remaining milk and lemon rind into the saucepan and bring to the boil. Reduce heat and add the drained rice to the milk. Mix well and allow to cook gently until the milk is almost absorbed and the rice is soft. Discard the lemon rind. Then stir in the sugar, butter and beaten egg yolk and mix well. Cook gently, sitirring occasionally, until the sugar, milk and egg yolk have been absorbed and the pudding is rich and creamy. Transfer to serving dish and sprinkle with cinnamon.

Serves 4.

BRAZO DE GITANO

Swiss Roll with Cream Filling

The Spanish version of Swiss roll goes by the colorful name of *brazo de gitano,* which literally means "gypsy's arm." Both the vanilla and chocolate flavored versions of this light sponge cake are popular all over Spain.

4 egg yolks
4 egg whites
1 tablespoon cornstarch/corn flour
½ cup all-purpose flour
¾ cup sugar
pinch salt
1 teaspoon baking powder
½ teaspoon vanilla extract/essence
confectioners'sugar for decoration
butter for greasing

Line a Swiss roll tin (approx. 11 inches long) with well greased wax paper.

Mix the flour with the cornstarch and baking powder, and sift three times. Set aside.

Beat the egg whites with a pinch of salt and 2 tablespoons of sugar until stiff.

In another bowl beat the egg yolks with the remaining sugar and vanilla until thick and creamy.

Fold the stiffened egg whites into the yolks.

Then fold in the well sifted flour and cornstarch.

Pour the mixture into the prepared tin, spread evenly and bake in a moderately hot oven for about 12 minutes.

Sprinkle a sheet of wax paper with confectioners' sugar. When the sponge is ready, turn it out onto the paper and remove the greased paper. Place a clean sheet of wax paper on top of the sponge and gently roll up along the long edge. Let cool.

When the cream filling is ready, unroll the sponge gently, remove the paper and spread evenly with the cream. Then roll up the cake once again and dust with a little more confectioners' sugar.

Cream Filling:
See recipe for crema pastelera below.

CREMA PASTELERA
Cream Filling

Crema pastelera is the Spanish version of the French *crème patissière.* It is extremely versatile as it can be used as a filling for cakes and tarts, and as a sweet in its own right, either served separetely or fried in batter or breadcrumbs (see *crema frita* p. 225).

3 egg yolks
2 cups milk
4 tablespoons sugar
2 teaspoons cornstarch/corn flour
2 teaspoons all-purpose flour
1 vanilla bean—broken into 4 pieces
rind of 1 lemon—peeled and cut into long strips
1 egg white

Reserve 2 tablespoons of the milk. Put the remaining milk, lemon rind and vanilla bean into a heavy saucepan and slowly bring to the boil. Remove from heat and cover for a few minutes.

Meanwhile, beat the egg yolks and the sugar in a large bowl until thick and creamy. Mix the sifted flour and cornstarch with the 2 tablespoons of cold milk and beat into the egg yolk mixture. Remove the vanilla stick and the lemon rind from the hot milk and discard. Beating constantly, slowly pour the hot milk into the egg mixture.

Pour the mixture back into the saucepan and cook very gently, stirring constantly, until the mixture just begins to boil and thicken.

Remove from heat. Whisk the egg white until stiff and fold it into the custard mixture. Cook over a low heat for about 2 minutes, occasionally stirring the mixture with a folding movement. Allow to cool.

BUÑUELITOS DE PLATANO

Banana Fritters

Buñuelitos are always a hit with adults and children alike, and the batter recipe given here produces extremely light fritters. *Buñuelitos* are often served at *merienda* time (tea time), especially when the family gathers to celebrate special occasions such as namedays, birthdays, or children's parties.

4-6 bananas
oil for frying
2 tablespoons sugar for dredging
½ teaspoon cinnamon

For the batter:

2 teaspoons sunflower oil
¼ cup water
2 tablespoons all-purpose flour
1 large egg
pinch of salt

To make the batter:

Put the sifted flour in a bowl with a pinch of salt; make a small well in the middle and add the water and oil. Gradually mix in the flour with a fork or spoon and stir until smooth. Put in the refrigerator for about half an hour. Then, beat the egg white until stiff and fold into the batter.

Cut each banana into three pieces and coat well with the batter.

Fry in deep hot oil until golden brown, turning once or twice, then drain. Combine the sugar and the cinnamon and sprinkle over the fritters.

Serves 4.

Variation:

Use firm, ripe apricots or plums. Carefully peel and destone the fruit, then fill the empty center with a little *queso fresco* (fromage frais), close with a blanched almond, dip into the batter and fry gently.

BUÑUELITOS DE MANZANA

Apple Fritters

Another variation of *buñuelitos* using apples and a little rum.

2-3 eating apples
1½ tablespoons rum
1 lemon
4 tablespoons sugar
2 tablespoons water
batter for coating
½ teaspoon cinnamon

Make batter as indicated in the recipe for *buñuelitos de plátano* in previous recipe.

Peel and core the apples. Cut into medium-thick slices, then coat them with lemon juice to prevent discoloration.

Put 1½ tablespoons sugar, water, rum and a few drops of lemon juice into a bowl and mix well. Add the apple slices and coat with the liquid. Leave for about 30 minutes, stirring occasionally.

Remove the apple slices, drain on a paper towel. Then

coat with the batter and fry in deep, hot fat until golden brown, turning once or twice.

Combine the remaining sugar and the cinnamon and sprinkle over the fritters.

Serves 4 to 5.

CHURROS

Crispy Fried Batter Rings

Churros are sold in bars and market places all over Spain. They are quite irresistible and are usually served at breakfast time with a cup of hot chocolate or coffee. In Spain a special *churros* maker called a *churrera* is used to produce the batter rings. However, a large but strong forcing bag should suffice if used with care—particularly when pressing the thick batter or dough out into the hot fat. The bag should not be filled more than three-quarters full and it is a good idea to practice first before pressing out the batter directly into the hot oil.

1½ cups water
2 cups all-purpose flour
pinch of salt
oil for frying (about 4 cups)
sugar for dredging

Put the water and salt in a saucepan and bring to the boil. Remove from heat and add the flour immediately. Mix constantly with a wooden spoon until the mixture forms a thick mass. Allow to cool for about 5 minutes.

Heat the oil in a deep frying pan until very hot.

Meanwhile, put the warm thick batter into a large strong bag or *churros* maker with a fluted nozzle with a diameter equivalent to the width of a small finger (about ¼ inch) and press out several rings of batter into the hot fat, cutting the batter with a sharp knife about every 6 inches. Allow the *churros* rings to cook for about 5 minutes, turning occasionally, until golden.

When cooked, remove the *churros* with a perforated spoon, drain on paper towel, sprinkle with sugar and serve immediately

Makes about 15 *churros* rings.

FLAN

Caramel Custard

This light custard is probably the most popular of all Spanish desserts, judging by its presence on the menus of most restaurants.

Caramel:

5 tablespoons sugar

Custard:

3 cups milk
3 large whole eggs (or 4 medium)
3 egg yolks
2-3 tablespoons sugar (to taste)
½-1 teaspoon vanilla extract/essence (to taste)

The Caramel:

Put the 5 tablespoons sugar in a small saucepan over a moderate heat and allow to melt. When it starts to change color, stir gently until the syrup becomes a deep golden brown. Pour the caramel into 6 small molds or one soufflé dish, moving the dish/molds quickly to coat the botton and sides with the caramel.

Put the eggs, egg yolks, sugar and vanilla extract into a large bowl and whisk. Heat the milk to boiling point, allow to cool for a minute or so, then pour the hot milk onto the egg mixture gradually.

Stir well, then pour the custard into the dish/molds.

Stand in a bain-marie or a roasting pan containing hot water, cover with wax paper and bake in a preheated, moderate oven until the custard is set (about 40 minutes).

When set, remove from the oven and wait until the custard is cold before turning out onto a serving dish.

Serves 6.

CREMA FRITA CON SALSA DE MELOCOTON O CIRUELA

Cream Fritters with Peach or Plum Sauce

Crema frita is a real delight. The small squares should be crispy on the outside and rich and creamy on the inside. A rather drier *crema pastelera* than normal is needed to facilitate handling and though some attention to detail is required to make good cream fritters, it is well worth the effort. The cream slices can be covered either in batter or breadcrumbs according to preference and then fried in deep oil. Cream fritters are delicious served sprinkled with sugar and/or accompanied by fruit sauce.

1½ cups milk
1 cup all-purpose flour
2 eggs
2 yolks
¼ cup granulated sugar
2 teaspoons butter
few drops vanilla extract/essence
1 vanilla bean
sugar for dredging
oil for frying

Batter (see recipe for Bueñlitos de Plátano)

Coating for breadcrumbs:
day-old white breadcrumbs
all-purpose flour
1 egg—beaten

Reserve 3 tablespoons of milk. Put the remaining milk in a saucepan with the vanilla stick and bring to the boil. Remove from heat and allow to cool for a few minutes. Discard the vanilla stick.

Meanwhile, put the sifted flour and granulated sugar into a bowl with the 4 egg yolks and 3 tablespoons of milk and beat until creamy.

Pour the warm milk into the egg mixture and mix well. Return the mixture to the saucepan and stir constantly until it reaches boiling point. Remove from heat and stir in the butter. Whisk the whites until stiff and gently fold into the cream. Bring to the boil once more, then allow to cool for a few minutes. Stir in a few drops of vanilla extract.

When cool, transfer the cream to a shallow dish and spread evenly to about 1½ inches in thickness. Place in the refrigerator for about 2 hours.

When completely set, cut into small squares or rounds. Ease out of the dish with a spatula knife. Then:

—if using batter, dip the cream into the batter;

—if using breadcrumbs, first dip in all-purpose flour, then in beaten egg and finally coat with breadcrumbs.

Heat the oil in a deep frying pan until hot, but not smoking and fry the coated cream slices until golden. Drain and serve immediately sprinkled with sugar and/or with hot plum or peach sauce.

Plum/Peach Sauce:

5-6 large ripe, but firm plums (or 4 medium peaches)
2 tablespoons rum
2 tablespoons sugar (or to taste)

Peel, stone and quarter the plums/peaches. Then cut into pieces.

Place the fruit and rum in a blender and process until

smooth. Transfer the fruit purée to a saucepan, add the sugar and heat gently until hot (do not boil).

Serve with the Cream Fritters.

LECHE FRITA
Fried Custard Squares

This is a less elaborate version of *crema frita.*

3 cups milk
3 tablespoons granulated sugar (or to taste)
rind of 1 lemon cut into long strips
2 eggs—beaten
5 tablespoons cornstarch/corn flour
fresh breadcrumbs for coating
½ cup oil for frying
sugar for dredging
½ teaspoon ground cinnamon

Mix the cornstarch to a thin paste with 5 tablespoons of cold milk.

Put the remaining milk, lemon rind and granulated sugar into a saucepan and bring to the boil. Remove the lemon rind and discard.

Then reduce heat slightly, add the cornstarch paste and stir until the mixture thickens. Pour the custard into a shallow dish (about 2 inches deep and 8 inches square). Allow to cool, then place in the refrigerator for 2-3 hours.

Cut the custard into squares, measuring about 1½ inches. Ease out of the dish with a spatula, then dip the squares into the beaten egg and coat them with breadcrumbs.

Heat the oil in a large frying pan. When very hot (but not smoking), fry about 5 or 6 of the squares for a couple of minutes on each side until golden. Drain and serve immediately, sprinkled with sugar and cinnamon.

Serves 4 to 6.

NATILLAS
Little Custard Creams

These little custards are served as a dessert in their own right, and are a great favorite with people of all ages.

3 cups milk
2 egg yolks
2 large whole eggs
3 tablespoons sugar
1 vanilla bean
rind of 1 lemon—cut into long strips
ground cinnamon

Put the milk, vanilla bean, 1 tablespoon of sugar and lemon rind in a heavy saucepan and bring to the boil. Remove from heat and discard the vanilla stick and lemon rind.

Put the egg yolks, the eggs and remaining sugar into a large bowl and whisk until smooth and creamy.

Beating constantly, slowly pour the hot milk onto the egg mixture. Pour the mixture back into the saucepan and cook very gently (do not allow to boil or the custard will curdle). Stir constantly until the custard thickens and coats the back of a spoon.

Pour into 4 individual dishes and, just before serving, sprinkle with ground cinnamon.

Serves 4.

PASTEL DE CASTAÑAS Y ALBARICOQUES
Chestnut and Apricot Cream

This rich sweet makes an ideal dinner party dessert.

4 tablespoons sweetened chestnut purée

¾ cup thick cream
2-3 ripe apricots
2 marron glacés (candied chestnuts)
2 egg whites
2 tablespoons brandy

Put the brandy and chestnut purée into a bowl and mix well. Reserve about a quarter of the cream and whip the rest until thick. Then mix the whipped cream with the chestnut purée in the bowl.

Peel, stone and coarsely chop the apricots and stir them into the purée.

Beat the egg whites until very stiff and fold them into the chestnut mixture. Spoon into four individual glass dishes and place in the refrigerator for an hour or two.

Before serving, whip the remaining cream until stiff, divide into 4 portions and pile on top of each individual dessert. Cut the marron glacés in half and place on top of the cream.

Serves 4.

Variation:

Omit the apricots and add about ½ lb of puréed fresh or frozen raspberries.

PASTEL DE MANZANA

Asturian Apple Crumble

There are many versions of this dessert from the apple and cider region of Spain. It can be served with *crema pastelera* or whipped cream.

The Crumble:

½ cup granulated sugar
1 cup all-purpose flour
3 tablespoons butter
1 egg

The Fruit:

2 level teaspoons ground cinnamon
1 teaspoon chopped fresh mint
1½ lb baking apples—peeled and cored
¼ cup brown sugar (or to taste)

Prepare the fruit by quatering the apples and cutting into medium-sized slices.

Combine the mint, cinnamon and brown sugar in a bowl. Add the apples and coat in the sugar mixture.

Grease the bottom and sides of an ovenproof pie or soufflé dish. Arrange the apples in layers in the greased dish, adding any of the brown sugar and cinnamon mixture left in the bowl.

Using your fingers, rub the butter into the flour and add the granulated sugar and mix. The mixture should resemble breadcrumbs. Add the egg and mix with two knives until the egg has been absorbed.

Cover the fruit with the flour mixture and press down firmly. Bake in a preheated, moderately hot oven for about 50 minutes, until the topping is crispy. Remove from oven and allow to cool.

Serves 4 to 6.

PESTIÑOS

Fried Honeyed Pastries

Pestiños are light honeyed pastries made with a type of choux paste and fried in hot oil. They are particularly popular in Andalusia, especially at Christmastime.

5 tablespoons water
2 tablespoons dry white wine
1½ cups all-purpose flour
1 tablespoon lard

1 tablespoon butter
4 tablespoons clear honey (or to taste)
oil for frying (about 4 cups)
multi-colored sugar sprinkles

Heat the water, wine, lard, butter and salt in a saucepan over a moderate heat. When the mixture starts to boil, remove from heat; add the flour all at once and mix well with a wooden spoon until the paste comes away from the sides of the pan. Do not continue beating after this point is reached.

Remove the paste and place on a well floured board. Knead well and form a ball shape. Set aside in a cool place for about an hour.

Using a rolling pin, roll out the paste very thinly. Then with a knife cut out several rectangle shapes, each measuring approx. 3½ x 6 inches. Pick up one corner of the pastry rectangle and roll it very loosely towards the other end. Then gently flatten the pastry. Dip a pastry brush in water and wet the outside corner flap so as to stick down the pastry and prevent the *pestiños* opening up when fried.

Put the oil in a deep frying pan and heat until very hot, but not smoking. Place the *pestiños*, two at a time, in the hot oil and fry until golden. Remove, drain and allow to cool.

Put the *pestiños* on a piece of wax paper and pour over the clear honey to taste. This will give a syrupy finish to the *pestiños*. Transfer to a serving dish. Sprinkle with multi-colored sugar sprinkles.

PUDÍN DE CAFE

Coffee Pudding

Pudín de café is a splendid dinner party dessert. It consists of a soft coffee meringue base covered with a rich custard cream sauce.

4 egg whites
1½ teaspoons instant coffee
6 tablespoons sugar
¼ cup slivered/flaked toasted almonds

For the cream topping:

2 egg yolks
1½ cups milk
3 tablespoons sugar
rind 1 lemon—cut into long strips
1 vanilla bean—broken into 4 pieces
½ teaspoon instant coffee
2 teaspoons cornstarch/corn flour
2 teaspoons all-purpose flour

To make the meringue:

Beat the egg whites until very stiff, fold in the sugar and the instant coffee. Grease a mold and fill with the egg white mixture. Cook in a double boiler (or place the covered mold in a saucepan and add enough water to reach halfway up side of mold) and simmer very gently for 40 minutes, taking care that pan does not run dry. Then remove, and place the mold in a preheated, moderate oven for 5-10 minutes until the meringue is golden and spongy.

Remove from the oven and allow to cool, then place upside down on a plate and remove the mold.

To make the cream:

Reserve 2 tablespoons of cold milk. Put the remaining milk, lemon rind, coffee and vanilla bean into a heavy saucepan and slowly bring to the boil. Remove from heat and cover for a few minutes.

Meanwhile, beat the egg yolks and the sugar in a bowl until thick and creamy. Mix the sifted flour and cornstarch with the cold milk and beat into the egg yolk mixture.

Remove the vanilla bean and lemon rind from the hot milk and discard.

Beating constantly, slowly pour the hot milk into the egg mixture. Pour the mixture back into the saucepan and cook very gently, still stirring constantly until the mixture begins to boil and thicken. Remove from heat. Allow to cool for about 5 minutes. Pour the cream over the meringue and sprinkle with flaked toasted almonds.

Delicious served straight away, and even better when refrigerated for 2 hours and eaten cold.

PUDIN DE HUEVOS NEVADOS CON CARAMELO
Caramel Snow Pudding

Pudín de huevos nevados con caramelo is another excellent dinner party sweet. It is almost the inverse of the previous dessert and has a creamy custard base topped with a caramelized soft meringue.

4 large egg yolks
4 egg whites
2 cups milk
1 heaped teaspoon cornstarch/corn flour
4 tablespoons sugar
¼ cup slivered/flaked toasted almonds

Caramel:
½ cup granulated sugar
4 tablespoons water

To make the custard base:

Put the milk into a heavy saucepan and bring to the boil. Meanwhile, place the sugar in a bowl and mix in the cornstarch, add the egg yolks and beat until smooth and creamy. Remove the milk from heat and gently pour onto the egg mixture, stirring constantly. Pour the mixture back into the heavy saucepan and cook the custard over a moderate heat, still stirring gently until the mixture thickens and coats the back of the spoon. Do not allow the custard to boil or it will curdle. Pour the custard into a shallow serving dish and allow to cool.

To make the soft meringue:
Beat the egg whites until very stiff. Then, in a large shallow pan, poach tablespoonfuls of egg white in simmering water (or milk, if preferred) until firm, Remove with a perforated spoon and place on top of the set custard. Sprinkle with almonds.

To make the caramel:
Dissolve the granulated sugar in the water over a low heat, then boil until the syrup becomes golden in color. When golden, pour over the almonds and meringue.

TOCINO DE CIELO
Sweet Egg Yolk Delight

Tocino is the white fatty part of bacon and this curious name *tocino de cielo* literally means "heavenly fatty bacon" or "fatty bacon from heaven." It is an extremely sweet and rich dessert made with a thick syrup and egg yolks and topped with a light caramel. Understandably, it is usually served in very small portions.

¾ cup sugar
1 cup cold water
5 yolks
1 whole egg
rind of 1 lemon—thinly peeled and cut into long strips
a little extra water

For the Caramel:
5 tablespoons sugar

First make the caramel by putting the 5 tablespoons sugar in a small saucepan and heating over a moderate heat until the sugar melts. When it starts to change color, stir gently until it becomes a deep golden brown. Pour the caramel into a medium-sized, shallow pie or flan dish, moving the dish quickly to coat the bottom and sides. Then, set aside.

Put the water into a saucepan together with the sugar and the lemon rind. Bring to the boil, then reduce heat to very low, stir and cook for about 15-20 minutes, stirring occasionally, to form a thick syrup. Remove the rind and allow the syrup to cool for about 10 minutes.

Beat the egg, egg yolks and 1 tablespoon of water in a bowl until well mixed and creamy. Stirring constantly with a wooden spoon, add the warm syrup little by little. Pour over the caramel in the pie or flan dish. Place a piece of wax paper on top and cover with a heavy lid.

Place the flan dish in a bain-marie (a large pan, containing warm water to a depth of about one-third of the pie dish). Heat gently to simmering point and allow to cook for about 10 minutes.

Then place the whole thing (bain-marie and flan) in a preheated, moderate oven for an additional 10 minutes. Remove from the oven and leave the flan to cool in the bain-marie.

When cool, loosen the sides of the *tocino de cielo* with a spatula and turn the sweet out onto a serving dish.

Serves 4 to 6.

THE WINES OF SPAIN

by P.C. Chitnis

SHERRY

Sherry is a wine with a history as long as that of *Jerez de la Frontera,* a town on the southernmost tip of Spain near the Straits of Gibraltar. The *Jerez* region has been famous since the sixteenth century for its production of world-class sherries and brandies, both aged in the unique *solera* system. Blending and maturing is a process that takes years, depending on the type and quality of wine in view. It is accomplished in a solera, a word derived from the Latin *solum,* or Spanish *suelo,* meaning a floor. Essentially, it consists of oak butts of 108 gallons capacity, subdivided into 'scales' or series of butts containing wine of identical type, but of progressively younger vintages. From time to time a limited amount of wine for bottling and final blending is withdrawn from the series of butts first laid down. These are replenished or 'refreshed' from butts of rather younger wine, which are in turn refreshed down all the scales of the *criadera,* or 'nursery.' The process is feasible because, in limited admixture, the younger wine rapidly takes on the character of the older. The number of scales varies according to the type of sherry. The most important difference between the making of sherry and most other wines is that sherry is fermented and matured with free access to the atmosphere, achieved by leaving a space in the cask above the liquid and only loosely stoppering it.

Varieties of Sherries

Fino

This dry wine from the Palomino grape variety is very light and pale gold in color, with a pungent but delicate aroma of almonds.

Manzanilla

Another dry wine from the Palomino grape, Manzanilla is lighter, paler and more delicate than fino, but lacking its aromatic complexity and structure.

Amontillado

Smooth and elegant on the palate, this wine is a more mature fino, with a deeper amber color and a characteristic bouquet and 'nutty' flavor.

Palo Cortado

Darker than Amontillado, this wine has the aroma of Amontillado and the structure and flavor of Oloroso.

Oloroso

Commonly used for dessert sherries, this deep mahogany wine offers the richness and intense aroma of a long aging process. A dry, deep and smooth sherry with a velvety finish.

Pale Cream

A fino wine with a distinct sweetness that comes from the addition of concentrated and rectified grape must.

Its pale gold color and delicate floral aromas make it very light and smooth on the palate.

Cream

This sweet Oloroso, shiny mahogany in color, combines the aromas of Oloroso wine with subtle hints of old oak and raisin. Slightly sweet, smooth and very pleasant.

Pedro Ximénez

A sweet wine of the Pedro Ximénez grape variety, with a dark mahogany color and amber aura. It has a complex and harmonious aroma full of subtleties, but in which the raisin flavor still dominates. A dense, velvety wine.

LA RIOJA

The Rioja wine district comprises some 43,000 hectares of vineyards on either side of the Ebro river in Northern Spain. Records of the legendary wines from this region date back to the Phoenicians, who pushed up the Ebro in their shallow draft boats. Six varieties of grapes are regularly used for making fine Riojas today:

Garnacho

These vines are vigorous and erect, mature rather late and produce medium-sized, thin-skinned black grapes—though depending on the method of cultivation the plant may produce white grapes. The musts yield wine high in alcohol (up to 15%) and also in tartaric acid. They are blended with the musts from other grapes to add lightness and alcoholic strength to Rioja wines.

Tempranillos

The variety of grape used to produce tempranillos are also robust, but mature about two weeks before the Garnachos. Their musts are less sweet than those of Garnachos, producing wines with from 10.5 to 13 % of alcohol with a good acid balance. Often used as the basis for fine red Riojas.

Graciano

These vines possess thinner shoots with grapes that mature later than the Tempranillos, and produce musts of only 10-12% alcohol.

Mazuelo

This commonly used black grape produces an alcoholic strength similar to that of the Tempranillo. It is rich in tannin and imparts long life to the wines in which it is blended.

All red Riojas are made from a careful blending and balance of different musts, achieved by mixing the grapes in appropriate proportions before fermentation. A typical blend for one of today's wines might be:

Tempranillo	50%
Garnacho	25%
Graciano	15%
Mazuelo	10%

As for the white grapes of the Rioja region, only two varieties are regularly employed in the wine-making process:

Malvasía

These vigorous and large-leafed vines produce grapes that are white, tinted with red when fully mature. They yield about 11% alcohol and are among the best of the white riojas, fresh and without acid reaction in the mouth.

Viura

More prolific than the Malvasías, Viura musts contain about the same amount of acid, but yield rather more alcohol to produce very pleasant white wines, lean and crisp, which readily complement elegant fare with pronounced flavors.

Varieties of Rioja Wines

Clarete

Light red wines of medium strength, bright color, and characteristic strong bouquet.

Tinto

Deeper in color, more full-bodied and of high alcoholic strength. Comparable to French Burgundies.

Rosado

Light, refreshing rosé wines, varying in dryness.

Blanco

White wines that are actually golden or greenish in color. They vary from sweet to dry, the best probably being the drier wines with a fresh, pebbly taste and good bouquet.

Reservas

Red wines of good vintage, aged over periods of years in oak casks.

OTHER WINE REGIONS IN SPAIN

Castilla y Leon is a large plateau in north central

Spain, where *Rueda* wines are produced. Refined and extremely dry with aromas of apple and pear, Rueda wines pair perfectly with Asian cuisine and spicy foods.

Toro, a region also in north-central Spain, produces deeply colored, robust red wines from Tempranillo and Garnacha grapes. These wines are wonderful accompaniments to beef, lamb and duck.

Navarra, in Northern Spain, has long been celebrated for its elegant rosado wines. This region is emerging as an innovator with its red wines, including fine blends of *Tempranillo* with Cabernet and Merlot.

The ***Penedés*** region, south of Barcelona near the Mediterranean coast, is celebrated for its sparkling wines, or Cava. Cava is a sophisticated wine with a crisp, fragrant flavor, ideal for a memorable toast or to complement seafood or spicy dishes.

SOME RECOMMENDATIONS

Sherries

González Byass, Tio Pepe Fino Sherry, Jerez

Best-selling Fino sherry of impeccable quality; dry, full-bodied, with delicate flavors. Aged for an average of five years in American oak barrels. A favorite tapas wine, Tio is also excellent with grilled seafood.

Emilio Lustau Escuadrilla, Rare Amontillado, Jerez

A dry, darker sherry with full-bodied and aromatic character. An excellent choice for rich tapas foods like mushrooms, foie gras, paté and toasted nuts.

Sanchez Romate Cream Sherry, Jerez

A darker cream sherry sweetened with a hint of Pedro Ximénez. A perfect pairing with cookies, pastries, and other desserts.

Red Riojas

Bodegas Paternina, Banda Azul, 1993, Rioja

Ernest Hemingway's favorite traditional Spanish Rioja. Bright ruby in color, with lush red fruits and soft tannins. Perfect with red meats and cheeses.

René Barbier, Mediterranean Merlot, 1993, Penedés

A full-bodied classic Bordeaux red. Its cherry character is accompanied by tones of clove and a note of oak. Rich tannins make this a good match for wild game or veal.

Compañía Vinícola del Norte de España (Cune), Reserva 1989, Rioja

An accessible fruity red wine with a richness and maturity produced by two years in oak and another two years of bottle aging. Serve with roasted or grilled meats, hearty stews, and tapas.

Bodegas Age, Siglo Crianza 1992, Rioja

Made from 50% Tempranillo, 35% Garnacho and 15% Mazuela grapes, this refined, full-bodied wine is a deep red with purple and golden highlights, a fruity bouquet and a light vanilla aroma. Wonderful match with red meat, venison, and cheese.

White Riojas

Marqués de Cáceres, Crianza, Rioja

Aged in French Tronçais oak casts for a touch of oak, this wine is also balanced with a fine fruity bouquet and good acidity. Produced from selected cuvées, it has excellent complexity and structure. A delightful aperitif, it is also paired well with shellfish, fish and beef prepared in sauce, sautéed vegetables, and mild cheeses.

Marqués de Cáceres, Satinela, Rioja

A slightly sweet wine made from Viura grapes with a small percentage of Malvasia. A fresh bouquet of apricot, peach and acacia flowers make it a refreshing aperitif as well as a wonderful accompaniment to sweet and sour dishes, curries, foie gras, feta cheese and light desserts.

Sparkling Wines

Freixenet, Cordón Negro Brut, Cava, Penedés

A dry medium-bodied sparkling wine with a fine mousse, clean flavors and a floral, fruity nose. Excellent with Caesar salad, white cheeses, seafood and spicy dishes, such as Mexican, Szechuan, or Thai.

Segura Viudas, Brut Reserva, Cava, Penedés

This fine sparkling wine is fairly crisp with an interesting floral note and sensation of creaminess. This classic Cava pairs well with seafood, fish dishes, and spicy cuisine.

Recipes in English

APPETIZERS
Carrots in Vinaigrette Dressing, 28
Cheese Bites, 27
Cucumber and Carrots in Sweet Pickle, 29
Stuffed Eggs, 25
Fritters
  Small Shrimp Fritters, 21
  variations, 22
Meat Balls, 19
  with Sherry Sauce, 19
Spanish Omelet (see Egg Dishes)
Paella (see Rice Dishes)
Peppers
  Peppers in Sweet Pickle, 30
  Baked Peppers and Tomatoes, 20
  Baked Peppers with Vinaigrette (see Vegetables)
  Fried Green Peppers, 25
Mini Pork Kebabs, 26
  with Peppers and Onions, 26
  variations, 27
Garlic Prawns/Shrimps, 24
Olives
  marinated, 18
  variations, 19
Russian Salad, 23
Sardines
  grilled, 23
Squid in its own ink sauce (see Fish)
Walnut Salad, 22

SOUPS
Cold Almond, Garlic and Grape Soup (White *Gazpacho*)
Clam Broth, 41
Cream of Carrot Soup, 53
Chicken Broth with Tidbits, 52
Crab Soup, 44
Simple Garlic Soup, 38
  Garlic Soup with Eggs (1), 39
  Garlic Soup with Eggs (2), 40
Fish Soup
  Saffron Fish Soup, 51
  Hot Fish *Gazpacho*, 35
Gazpacho
  Andalusian Cold Salad Soup (*Gazpacho*), 34
  Cold Almond, Garlic and Grape Soup (White *Gazpacho*), 37
  Hot Fish *Gazpacho*, 35
  Hot *Gazpacho*, Cadiz-Style, 36
Lentil Soup, Madrid-Style, 46
  variations, 47
Chilled Cream of Melon Soup,

48
Noodle Soup "in an Instant," 46
Potato Soup, 52
Andalusian Pumpkin Soup, 42
"Quater of an Hour" Soup, 45
Vegetable Soup with Croutons and Mint, 49
Watercress, Lettuce and Parsley Soup, 43
variations, 43

STEWS

Maria Luisa's Bean and Cabbage Stew with Tripe, 57
Asturian Bean and Sausage Soup, 59
Galician Bean and Turnip Soup, 58
variations, 59
Boiled Chicken, Meat and Vegetables (Cocido madrileño), 55
Rapid Chick-pea Stew, 61

VEGETABLES

Beans
Broad Beans with Sausage, Catalan Style, 72
Green Beans with Ham, 73
Green Beans with Vinaigrette, 74
Cabbage
Red Cabbage, Orange and Walnut Salad, 75
Celery
Celery in Tomato Sauce, 63
Eggplant/Aubergine
Eggplant/Aubergine with Ham and White Sauce, 66
Eggplant/Aubergine with Mushrooms and Tomatoes, 68
Fried Eggplants/Aubergines, 66
Leeks
Leeks Gratin, 81
Leeks with Ham in White Sauce, 81
Mushrooms
Mushrooms in Garlic Sauce, 69
Mushrooms in Sherry Sauce, 70
Potatoes
Potatoes in Parsley Sauce, 76
Widowed Potatoes, 77
Potato Fritters filled with White Sauce, 75
Mallorca-Style Potato Salad, 71
Peas
Peas with Ham, 74
Pears
Pears with Green Mayonnaise, 78
Peppers
Roasted Red Peppers with Vinaigrette, 79
Stuffed Peppers with Tomato Sauce, 64
Stewed Vegetables (*Pisto*), 80
Zucchini/Courgettes
Zucchini/Courgettes Gratin, 69

RICE DISHES

Boiled Rice with Green Beans and Tomato Sauce, 88
Boiled Rice with Tomato, Onion and White Wine Sauce, 88
Boiled Rice with Tomato Sauce, 87
Drunken Scampi with Rice, 91
Paella a la Valenciana, 84
variations, 86
Rice with Cauliflower and Red Sausage, 89
Rice with Chicken, 90
Saffron Rice, 86
Simple Rice and Tuna Salad, 93
Valencian Rice Salad, 92
variations, 92

EGG DISHES

Baked Eggs
Baked Eggs with Vegetables, Ham and Sausage, 95
Baked Snow Eggs, with Grated Cheese and Ham (and variations), 100
Fried Eggs
Fried Eggs, Spanish-Style, 98
Cuban-Style Fried Eggs, 98
Valencian-Style Fried Eggs, 98
Hard-Boiled Eggs
Hard-Boiled Eggs Mimosa, 97
Hard-Boiled Eggs with White Sauce, 97
Scrambled Eggs
Scrambled Eggs, Peppers and Tomatoes (*Piperrada*), 101
Spanish Omelet
Spanish Potato Omelet, 103
Potato and Asparagus Omelet, 103
Potato, Pepper and Chorizo Omelet, 104
Potato and Tuna Omelet, 104
Stuffed Eggs
Fried Stuffed Eggs, with Tomato Sauce, 99

FISH AND SHELLFISH
Bream (or Red Snapper)
Baked Bream, 114
Bream in Cider, 115
Brill
Baked Brill in White Wine, 141
Brill with Courgettes/Zucchini, 143
Cod
Baked in Salt, 110
Basque Style, 111
Cod or Haddock, Basque-Style (*Chiorro*), 122
in Parsley Sauce, 112
Salt Cod with Tomatoes, 113
Fish Pie, 136
variations, 137
Fish Stew (see *Zarzuela*)
Grouper
Grouper in *Oloroso* Sherry, 132
Hake
Hake, Basque-Style, 131
Hake Pudding, 137
Hake in Tomato and Almond Sauce, 129
Herrings
Soused Herrings, 150
Mackerel
Stuffed with Apples and Sultanas, 115
Monkfish
Monkfish in Almond Sauce, 138
Monkfish with Tangy Sauce, 139
Mussels
How to clean mussels/clams, 127
Lemon Steamed Mussels, 127
Mussels with Wine, Garlic, Onion and Tomato Sauce, 128
Pickled Fish, 151
Porgy (*Urta*)
Porgy in Brandy, 146
Prawns (see Shrimps)
Mushrooms and Prawns/Shrimps "Rápido," 144
Red Snapper (see Bream)
Sea Bass, 126
Sea Bass in Red Sauce
Shark (see Tope)
Shellfish (see *Zarzuela*)
Shrimps/Prawns
Mushrooms and Shrimps/Prawns "Rápido,"

144
Skate
Skate Valencian Style, 140
Sole
Sole Alfonso XIII (with stuffed eggplants/aubergines), 123
Sole with Sherry and Spices, 124
Stuffed Fillet of Sole, 125
Squid
How to clean squid, 94
Granny's Squid with Leeks, 116
Squid in Its Own Ink Sauce, 118
Squid Surprise, 117
Swordfish
Swordfish with Asparagus and Potatoes, 133
Swordfish with Cucumber and Saffron Cream Sauce, 134
Swordfish with "Happy" Topping, 135
Tope (or Baby Shark)
Fried Marinated Tope: "It tastes good to me" (*Bienmesabe*), 120
Tope with Tomatoes, 119
Trout, 145
Trout with Cured Ham and Almonds, 145
Navarre-Style Trout, 144
Tuna
Tuna and Avocado Mousse, 108
"Onioned" Tuna (and variations), 105-106
Tuna Fish Fiesta, 107
Tuna Pie, 106
Zarzuela
Fish Stew Operetta, 147
Operetta of Sea Food, 148

MEAT

Beef
Beef and Celery Casserole, 177
Braised Steak, Galician-Style (and variation), 178
Fillet Steaks with Ham, Mushrooms and Onions, 175
Fillet Steaks with Sherry and Mustard (and variations), 176
Meat and Potato Stew (see Variation of Braised Steak, Galician-Style), 179
Oxtail Stew, 180
Pot Roast, Saragossa-Style, 179
Kidneys in Sherry Sauce, 170

Lamb and Kid
Braised Kid, Country-Style, 164
Braised Lamb, Andalusian-Style, 165
Kidneys in Sherry Sauce, 170
Lamb Cutlets, Navarre-Style, 166
Lamb in Tomato Sauce, 167
Roast Leg of Spring Lamb, 168
Roast Leg of Lamb, Aragonese-Style, 169
Oxtail Stew, 180

Pork
Asturian-Style Pork Fillets, 160
Braised Pork Chops with Puréed Spinach, 159
Cured Pork Loin Steaks with Plum Sauce, 162
Glazed Spare Ribs, Extremaduran-Style, 155
Pork Fillet with Celery and

Red Peppers, 154
Pork with Prunes, 161
Rioja-Style Pork Chops, 158
Roast Suckling Pig, 156
Roast Suckling Pig with Sherry and Sultana Sauce, 159
Sausage with Onions and Red Wine, 163
Tripe, Madrid-Style, 153

Veal

Veal Escalopes, Seville-Style, 171
Veal Escalopes in Sherry and Almond Sauce, 173
Veal Escalopes with Sweet Sherry, 174
Veal Escalopes, Valencia-Style, 172

POULTRY AND GAME

Duck

Duckling with Pine Nuts, Limes and Grapes—A House Speciality, 184
(and variations), 186
Roast Duckling, Andalusian-Style, 183
Roast Wild Duck with Cucumber and Raspberry Sauce, 186

Chicken

Aragonese-Style Chicken, 191
Chicken Breasts, Asturian-Style, 192
Chicken Breasts in Breadcrumbs, 189
Chicken Breasts in Orange and Mint Sauce, 190
Chicken "Hodgepodge" with Almonds, 188
Garlic Chicken, 191

Partridge

Partridge with Cider and Grapes (and variations), 201
Roast Partridge with Cucumber and Orange Sauce, 199
Stewed Partridge, 198

Pigeon

Braised Pigeon, 202

Quail

Quail in Pepper Nests, 197
Roast Quail, 196

Rabbit

Rabbit Casserole with Olives, 203

Turkey

Braised Turkey Breasts Macedonia, 195
Turkey with Asparagus, Ham and Chestnuts, 193

SAUCES

Ali Oli, 208
Almond Sauce (1), 205
Almond Sauce (2), 205
Green Sauce (1), 213
Green (Parsley) Sauce (2), 214
Mushroom Sauce, 207
Mayonnaise, 208
Garlic Mayonnaise (*ali oil*), 208
Green Mayonnaise (1), 210
Green Mayonnaise (2), 210
Green Mayonnaise (3), 211
Parsley Sauce (see Green Sauce 2)
Pepper and Almond Sauce (*Romescu*), 211
Tomato Sauce, 212
Vinaigrette Sauce (Basic), 29, 74, 215
Vinaigrette Sauce (2), 215
White Sauce, 67, 206

DESSERTS/CAKES/PASTRIES

Asturian Apple Crumble, 229
Caramel Custard, 224
Caramel Snow Pudding, 233

Chestnut and Apricot Cream (and variations), 228
Coffee Pudding, 231
Cream Fritters with Peach or Plum Sauce, 225
Cream Filling, 220
Crispy Fried Batter Rings (*Churros*), 223
Fried Custard Squares, 227
Fried Honeyed Pastries (*Pestiños*), 230
Fritters (with fruit)
  Apple Fritters, 222
  Banana Fritters (and variations), 221-222
Little Custard Creams, 228
Rice Pudding, Spanish-Style, 218
Sweet Egg Yolk Delight, 234
Swiss Roll with Cream Filling, 219

MISCELLANEOUS
Cleaning Mussels/Clams, 127
Cleaning Squid, 94
Migas (Croutons), 50
Sofrito (thick vegetable and meat sauce), 96

Recipes in Spanish

TAPAS
Aceitunas
en escabeche, 18
and variations, 19
Albondigas
con salsa de jerez, 19
Asadillo, 20
Bocaditos de queso, 27
Buñuelitos
de camarones, 21
and variations, 22
Calamares en su tinta (*see* Pescados)
Callos a la madrileña (*see* Carnes)
Carne con patatas (*see* Carnes)
Champiñones
Champiñones al jerez (*see* Verduras)
Champiñones al ajillo (*see* Verduras)
Ensaladilla
Ensaladilla de nueces, 22
Ensaladilla rusa, 23
Gambas al ajillo, 24
Huevos rellenos, 25
Paella (*see* Arroz)
Pepinos y zanahorias en escabeche dulce, 29
Pimientos
Pimientos asados con vinagreta (*see* Verduras), 25
Pimientos en escabeche dulce, 30
Pimientos fritos, 25
Pinchos
de cerdo, 26
and variations, 27
Sardinas asadas, 28
Tortilla (*see* Huevos)
Zanahorias aliñadas, 28
SOPAS
Crema de melón, 48
de zanahorias, 53
Gazpacho
Gazpacho andaluz, 34
Gazpacho caliente gaditano, 36
Gazpachuelo caliente de pescado, 35
Sopa de ajo blanco con uvas, 37
de ajo sencilla, 38
de ajo con huevos (1), 39
de ajo con huevos (2), 40
de almejas, 41
andaluza de calabaza, 42
de berros, lechuga y perejil (*and variations*), 43

de cangrejo, 44
al cuarto de hora, 45
de fideos al minuto, 46
de lentejas a la madrileña (*and variations*), 46
de menestra con migas y yerbabuena, 49
de patatas, 51
de pescado al amarillo, 51
de picadillo, 52

POTAJES

Berza María Luisa, 57
Caldo gallego, 58
variation: Pote gallego, 59
Cocido madrileño, 55
Fabada asturiana, 59
Guiso rápido de garbanzos, 61

VERDURAS

Apio en salsa de tomate, 63
"Bandera española," 64
Berenjenas
fritas, 66
con jamón y bechamel, 66
con setas y tomate, 68
Calabacines gratinados, 69
Champiñones
al ajillo, 69
al jerez, 70
Ensalada de patatas mallorquinas, 71
Frituras de patatas con bechamel, 75
Guisantes salteados con jamón, 74
Habas a la catalana, 72
Judías verdes
salteadas con jamón, 73
con vinagreta, 73
Lombarda con naranjas y nueces, 75
Patatas
en salsa verde, 76
viudas, 77
Ensalada de patatas mallorquinas, 71
Frituras de patatas con bechamel, 75
Peras con mayonesa verde, 78
Pimientos
asados con vinagreta, 79
"Bandera española," 64
Pisto (*Stewed Vegetables*), 80
Puerros
con jamón y bechamel, 81
gratinados, 81

ARROZ

Arroz
con azafrán, 86
blanco con tomate, 87
blanco con tomate, cebolla y vino blanco, 88
blanco con tomate y judías verdes, 88
con coliflor y chorizo, 89
con pollo, 90
Cigalas emborrachadas con arroz, 91
Ensalada
de arroz valenciana (*and variations*), 84
sencilla de arroz y atún, 93
Paella a la valenciana
and variations, 84

HUEVOS

Frituras de huevos rellenos con salsa de tomate, 99
Huevos a la flamenca, 95
Huevos duros
con bechamel, 97
mimosas, 97
Huevos fritos
a la española, 98
a la cubana, 98
a la valenciana, 98
Huevos nevados al plato con queso y jamón (*and variations*), 100
Huevos rellenos (*see* Tapas), 25

Piperrada (*Scrambled Eggs, Peppers and Tomatoes*), 101
Tortilla
  de patatas, 103
  de patatas y espárragos, 103
  de patatas, pimiento y chorizo, 104
  de patata y atún, 104
PESCADOS Y MARISCOS
Atún
  encebollado (*and variations*), 105
  Fiesta de atún, 107
  Manjar de atún y aguacate, 108
  Pastel de atún, 106
Arenques
  en escabeche, 150
Bacalao
  en salsa al horno, 110
  en salsa verde, 112
  con tomates, 113
  a la vizcaína, 111
Besugo
  al horno, 110
  en sidra, 115
Bienmesabe (*see* Cazón en adobo), 120
Caballas
  rellenas de manzanas y pasas, 115
Calamares
  con puerros: de abuela, 116
  en su tinta, 118
  Sorpresa de calamares, 117
Cazón
  con tomate, 119
  en adobo/Bienmesabe, 120
Cigalas emborrachadas con arroz (*see* Arroz), 91
Chiorro (*Cod or Haddock, Basque-Style*), 122
Escabeche de pescado, 151
Fiesta de atún, 107
Gambas
  al ajillo (*see* Tapas), 24
  Salteado rápido de champiñones y gambas, 144
Lenguado
  Lenguado Alfonso XIII, 123
  al jerez con especies, 124
  Lenguados rellenos, 125
Lobina
  en salsa colorada, 126
Manjar de atún y aguacate, 108
Mariscos
  Zarzuela de mariscos, 149
Mejillones
  con limón al vapor, 127
  a la marinera (*and variations*), 128
Merluza en salsa de tomate y almendras, 129
  a la vasca, 131
  Pudín de merluza, 131
Mero
  al oloroso, 132
Pastel de atún, 106
Pez espada
  con espárragos y patatas, 133
  con capa alegre, 135
  con pepino y crema de azafrán, 134
Pudín de merluza, 131
Pudín de pescado (*and variations*), 136
Rape
  en salsa de almendras, 138
  con salsa fuerte, 139
Raya
  valenciana, 140
Rodaballo
  con calabacines, 143
  con vino blanco al horno, 144
Salteado rápido de champiñones y gambas, 144
Sorpresa de calamares, 117
Trucha

a la navarra, 144
con jamón y almendras, 145
Urta al coñac, 146
Zarzuela de pescado, 147
de mariscos, 149

CARNES
Callos a la madrileña, 153

Cerdo
Cinta de cerdo con acelgas y pimiento, 154
Costillas a la extremeña, 155
Cochinillo asado, 156
Cochinillo asado con salsa de jerez y pasas, 157
Chuletas de cerdo a la riojana, 158
Culetas de cerdo con espinacas, 159
Filetes de cerdo a la asturiana, 160
Lomo ahumado en salsa de ciruelas, 162
Lomo de cerdo con ciruelas pasas, 161
Salchichas con cebollas y vino tinto, 163

Cordero y Cabrito
Cabrito al cortijo, 164
Cordero al amarillo, 165
Chuletas de cordero a la navarra, 166
Guiso de cordero con tomate, 167
Pierna de cordero a la aragonesa, 169
Pierna de cordero pascual asada, 168
Riñones al jerez, 170
Salchichas con cebollas y vino tinto, 163
Rabo de toro, 180
Riñones al jerez, 170

Ternera y Vaca
Escalope de ternera a la sevillana, 171
Escalope de ternera a la valenciana, 172
Escalope de ternera con salsa de jerez y almendras, 173
Escalope de ternera con vino dulce, 174
Filetes de solomillo con jamón, champiñones y cebollas, 175
Filetes de solomillo con jerez y mostaza (and variations), 176
Guiso de carne con acelga, 177
Guiso de carne con patatas, 179
Guiso de carne gallego, 178
Redondo guisado zaragozano, 179
Rabo de toro, 180

AVES Y CAZA

Codornices
asadas, 196
en pimientos, 197

Conejo
Guiso de conejo con aceitunas, 203

Gallina (*see* **Pollo**)

Pato
asado a la andaluza, 183
pinar serrano (*and variations*), 184
silvestre con salsa de pepino y frambuesa, 186

Pavo
con espárragos, jamón y castañas, 193
en salsa de macedonia al horno, 195

Perdices

estofadas, 198
con salsa de pepino y naranja, 199
con sidra y uvas (*and variations*), 201
Pichones
estofados, 202
Pollo/Gallina
Gallina en pepitoria, 188
Pechugas de pollo empanadas, 189
Pechugas de pollo en salsa de naranja y yerbabuena, 190
Pollo al ajillo, 191
Pollo a la chilindrón, 191
Pollo ovetense, 192
SALSAS
Ali Oli, 208
Mayonesa, 208
verde (1), 210
verde (2), 210
verde (3), 211
Romescu, 211
Salsa de almendras (1), 205
de almendras (2), 206
de bechamel, 206
de champiñones, 207
de tomate, 212
verde (1), 214
verde (2), 215
vinagreta sencilla, 215
vinagreta (2)
POSTRES Y PASTELES
Arroz con leche, 218
Brazo de gitano, 219
Buñuelitos
de albaricoque, 222
de ciruela, 222
de manzana, 222
de plátano, 221
Crema frita con salsa de melocotón o ciruela, 225
Crema pastelera, 220
Churros, 223
Flan, 224
Leche frita, 227
Natillas, 228
Pastel
de castañas y albaricoques (*and variations*), 228
de manzana, 229
Pestiños, 230
Pudín
de café, 231
de huevos nevados con caramelo, 233
Tocino de cielo, 234
MISCELANEA
Manera de limpiar los calamares (*Cleaning Squid*), 94
Manera de limpiar los mejillones/las almejas (*Cleaning Mussels/Clams*), 127
Migas, 50
Sofrito, 96